THE MAGIMIX AND
FOOD PROCESSOR
COOKERY BOOK

The Magimix and food processor cookery book

Marika Hanbury Tenison

ILLUSTRATED BY VAL BIRO

ictc

Published by **ICTC** Ltd
25 Lower Square
Isleworth, Middlesex UK

First Impression 1978 by
Hutchinson Benham
Second Impression 1978
Third Impression 1978
Fourth Impression 1978
Fifth Impression 1979
Sixth Impression 1980 by
ICTC Ltd
Text © Wellglen Properties Ltd 1978
Illustrations © Wellglen Properties Ltd 1978
Set in Monophoto Apollo by
Oliver Burridge Filmsetting Ltd, Crawley

Printed in Great Britain by
Chorley & Pickersgill Ltd of Leeds

ISBN 0 09 131940 4

Contents

Foreword

The kitchen gadget market is flooded with electrical machines for helping the housewife to liquidize, purée, chop, slice or grate. They come in all shapes and sizes and vary in price from one machine to another. During the last ten years I have been writing cookery books and cookery articles and have tried most of these machines and in fact, have used one or other of them in my kitchen until, at last, I found the Magimix food processor. Since that day the Magimix food processor has been the only machine of this kind I have used and I use it, on average, about twenty times a day or more in the course of my normal, everyday cooking for my family and friends and for testing recipes.

The Magimix food processor is stronger than other machines, it also takes up less space, is easier to clean, more reliable and attractively workmanlike to look at. With the Magimix food processor even the most inexperienced of cooks can produce beautiful food in a fraction of the time it would take her to prepare it by hand; culinary success is almost guaranteed and the everyday chores of cookery become a pleasure. Mixing, puréeing, chopping, grinding, cutting, slicing and shredding are all a matter of seconds instead of hard work and the results inspire the cook to attempt a much wider and more exciting range of dishes.

Writing this book gave Clare O'Connor and me great pleasure. It was hard work but, with the Magimix food processor as our third partner, we enjoyed every minute, coming up with ways to make both traditional recipes and a whole collection of new, original dishes we feel will suit any occasion. Hundreds of cooks in all categories have asked for this book and I sincerely hope that it will provide recipes that everyone will enjoy and which will help you make the best possible use of your Magimix processor – a machine that I believe to be the very best of its kind.

MARIKA HANBURY TENISON
CLARE O'CONNOR
Maidenwell, Cornwall 1977.

Introduction

Let your Magimix food processor help you make all your favourite recipes

In this book we have tried to cover as wide a field of recipes for all occasions as possible but there will, no doubt, be still more recipes you will wish to make with the help of your Magimix food processor.

Remember that if a recipe calls for mincing (grinding), mixing, beating (except in the case of egg whites), chopping, slicing or grating, all these processes can be done in your Magimix food processor in half the time it would take you to do them by hand.

Carefully go through the recipes you wish to adapt in order to get the full benefit from your Magimix food processor. Decide which ingredients can be prepared in the Magimix food processor and which sections of the method can be mixed, beaten or combined in the Magimix food processor before beginning your preparation.

Chopping If a recipe calls for chopped herbs, do this first of all in the Magimix food processor as herbs require a dry bowl. Hard ingredients like carrots will need a longer processing time than softer ingredients such as breadcrumbs, so work this out before starting to cut down on preparation time.

Slicing Slice the ingredients before processing those that require to be chopped as any sliced ingredients remaining in the bowl will be neatly incorporated into chopped ingredients.

Mincing (grinding)   Any ingredients which call for being minced (ground) can be processed in only seconds in your Magimix food processor using the metal blade – no more setting up or washing up of complicated machines and no more loss of valuable juices through the squeezing out process done by a mincing (grinding) machine.

Grating   Grating of cheese or vegetables is done in a flash with your Magimix grating disc in position.

Beating   Many sauces and sweets call for ingredients to be whisked while, at the same time, a hot liquid is being poured onto them. With your Magimix food processor this usually complicated procedure is made simple, merely put your basic ingredients in the Magimix bowl with the metal blade, set the machine in motion and pour the liquid in a steady stream through the feed tube.
   The metal blade or plastic blade can also be used to mix or blend ingredients together.

Pastry   Whatever kind of pastry you wish to make can be made with better results and great time saving in the Magimix food processor. Follow one of the recipes in this book substituting your own special balance of ingredients.

Cake making   Cakes and biscuits can be made in minutes with the help of your Magimix food processor, check the procedure with one of the basic recipes in this book.

Puréeing   Puréeing of soups or vegetables is done efficiently and incredibly quickly using the metal blade.

Adapting other recipes to prepare in your Magimix food processor

Use your Magimix food processor for any of your favourite recipes that require chopping, slicing, shredding, mincing, puréeing, blending, mixing or grating. Use your Magimix food processor for pastry, bread, biscuit and cake making. Let your Magimix food processor beat your eggs for you, purée fruit or vegetable mixes and process meat and other ingredients to the required consistency.
   In order not to wash out your Magimix bowl between processing ingredients, read through your recipe before beginning preparation and work out the order in which to process the ingredients.

Herbs should be chopped in a clean dry bowl so process these before getting to work on other ingredients. Breadcrumbs should be made in a clean dry bowl. Cheese should be reduced to crumbs in a clean dry bowl and so should nuts and other dry ingredients.

If you plan to chop ingredients in the Magimix bowl and then incorporate other ingredients, be careful not to over-process the first ingredients before adding the rest.

Remember that your Magimix food processor is an extremely sensitive, powerful machine that processes ingredients in seconds. It works to a touch and leaving it to run without supervision can result in ingredients being over-processed.

In my experience there are very few recipes which the Magimix food processor cannot help you make. With this versatile aid in your kitchen your favourite and newly discovered recipes will be made in half the time they would normally take and with the best possible results.

A basic Guideline to using your Magimix food processor

Almonds   Finely chopped, ground or sliced almonds can be a boon to a great many sweet and savoury dishes. Chop, grind or slice almonds with your Magimix food processor. Brown chopped almonds in a hot oven to sprinkle over sweet dishes to add attraction and a pleasant crunchy texture. Use ground almonds in place of flour in many cake, biscuit and sweet or savoury recipes. Sliced or slivered almonds can be browned in the oven or added to risottos and pilaus to give flavouring and texture.

Anchovies   Make your own gentleman's relish by processing anchovies with some butter in the Magimix bowl using the metal blade until a smooth paste is formed. Serve it on hot toast for tea or as an accompaniment to soups.

Add finely chopped anchovies to pasta sauces and some meat or poultry dishes to give a salty taste that is surprisingly un-fishy.

Apples   Remember that cut apples turn brown when exposed to the air so sprinkle the fruit with a little lemon juice or cover them with a solution of cold water mixed with lemon juice as soon as they have been peeled or sliced. Slice apples with the slicing blade. Chop apples for

11

salads with the metal blade. Purée cooked apples in the Magimix bowl using the metal blade. Make fresh apple juice with the juice extractor.

Apricots   Cooked fresh or dried apricots make a delicious purée to use as a base for puddings. Purée the cooked fruit in the Magimix bowl using the metal blade.

Fresh apricots can be sliced with the slicing disc and dried on absorbent paper in a low oven until the slices are leathery and pliable. Cool and store in a cool dry place.

Artichokes, Globe   Make delicious fillings or sauces for stuffing or serving with your globe artichokes in your Magimix food processor.

Artichokes, Jerusalem   Purée artichokes cooked in milk to make the base of a delicious soup. Slice or chop artichokes to cook as vegetables (especially good sliced and roasted).

Aubergines   Purée cooked aubergines with the metal blade to make a delicious starter. Slice raw aubergines to make into fritters or to fry until crisp. Chop aubergines to add to ratatouille and other mixed vegetables.

Avocados   Mash avocados to a purée with the Magimix metal blade to make the base of an avocado pâté, mousse or soup.

Bacon   Chop raw or cooked bacon with the metal blade to use as a garnish for soups, main courses and salads.

Bananas   Sprinkle peeled bananas with lemon juice to prevent them turning brown and slice them with the Magimix slicing blade or purée them with the metal blade for use in puddings.

Batter   Make all batters in the Magimix bowl using the metal blade. Put the flour and eggs into the bowl, switch on and gradually pour in the liquid required through the feed tube.

Beans, broad   Purée cooked broad beans with the metal blade to make a really delicious summer soup.

Beans, runner   Purée old runner beans with the metal blade to make a good vegetable accompaniment to rich main courses.

Beef   Inexpensive cuts of meat, finely chopped in your Magimix food processor with the metal blade will make

12

the base of many excellent recipes requiring minced or ground beef. Chop cooked beef in your Magimix food processor with the metal blade for all recipes requiring minced or ground cooked beef.

Beetroot Purée cooked beetroot with your metal blade to make the basis of an excellent Bortsch soup. Chop cooked beetroot with the Magimix metal blade to incorporate in both cold and hot dishes. Slice cooked beetroot with the slicing disc for salads and hot vegetable dishes. Grate raw beetroot with the grating disc to add colour to salads. Beetjuice can be extracted from raw or cooked beetroots by processing the vegetables through the juice extractor.

Berries Purée berries, raw or cooked, in the Magimix food processor using the metal blade. Slice firm straw-berries with the slicing disc to use in fruit salads. Use the juice extractor to get the most juice out of your berry fruit.

Biscuits Make your favourite biscuits in the Magimix food processor using your metal blade and following the method of one of the basic biscuit recipes in this book.

Bloaters Make an inexpensive bloater pâté by combining softened butter, filleted bloaters and seasoning in your Magimix bowl and using the metal blade. Add a little cream at the last minute and chill before serving.

Brandy butter Your Magimix food processor will make your traditional brandy or rum butter to go with the Christmas pudding and mince pies in only seconds. Use the metal blade.

Breadcrumbs Use up all those ends of stale bread to make fresh or brown breadcrumbs. Remove the crusts of stale white bread and process bread with the metal blade until they are reduced to fine crumbs. Store in an airtight jar. Bake crusts of white bread in a low oven until they are crisp and golden brown. Process the rusks in the Magimix food processor with the metal blade until they are reduced to fine crumbs. Cool and store in an airtight jar.

Bread dough Get 100 per cent success by making your bread dough in the Magimix bowl using the metal blade. No more kneading by hand, the machine will do it all for you.

Bread sauce   Make the fresh white breadcrumbs for a bread sauce in your Magimix food processor using the metal blade.

Brussels sprouts   Cook old sprouts and purée them in the Magimix food processor using the metal blade as a base for a well flavoured vegetable purée or an unusual winter soup.

Butter   Cream butter in your Magimix food processer using the metal blade for cakes and biscuit recipes.

Buttercreams for icing and filling cakes   Your Magimix food processor will produce a smooth and creamy buttercream filling or icing in only seconds. Use the metal blade and follow your favourite recipe or one of the suggestions in this book (see page 187).

Cabbage   Shred cabbage through the slicing blade for cooking and salads.

Cakes   The Magimix food processor makes quicker, lighter cakes than any you can make by hand. Follow the instructions given for the recipes in this book or adapt one of your favourite recipes.

Carrots   One of the most versatile and useful of winter vegetables. Slice, chop or grate them in the Magimix food processor to use in soups, sauces, casseroles and stews and for salads. Carrot juice can be extracted through the juice extractor.

Casseroles   Chop or slice all your vegetables in the Magimix food processor to incorporate into your casseroles. Finely chop herbs too, if they are to be added to the casserole at the last minute.

Cauliflower   Make the sauces for your cauliflower in your Magimix food processor and purée cooked cauliflower with the metal blade to make a delicious base for a soup.

Celeriac   Peel and roughly chop celeriac and blanch it in boiling water to which a tablespoon of lemon juice has been added to prevent it discolouring. Purée cooked celeriac with the metal blade to produce excellent vegetable soup or the base of a warming, aromatic winter soup or grate parboiled celeriac to add to salads.

Celery   Chop crisp celery with the metal blade to add to soups, stews and casseroles or slice it with the slicing disc to add to salads. Use the juice extractor to extract deliciously flavoured celery juice for adding to soups, stews or casseroles or for just drinking by itself when you need a pick-up.

Cheese   Never throw another heel of cheese away. Grate stale cheese or process it with the metal blade until the texture resembles fine breadcrumbs. Finish cheese sauces in your Magimix food processor, using the metal blade, for a smoother, finer consistency and make perfect cheese ice creams, cheese soufflés and many other cheese recipes.

Chicken   Chop up raw or cooked chicken in your Magimix food processor using the metal blade to form the base of hundreds of exciting recipes.

Chives   Chop chives in your Magimix bowl (make sure it is clean and dry before processing herbs).

Chopping   All fine or coarse chopping of ingredients can be done in the Magimix bowl using the metal blade.

Choux pastry   Put your flour into the Magimix bowl with the metal blade. Add boiling water and lard and process until the mixture forms a ball around the knife in the centre. Add the eggs, one by one, through the feed tube, with the Magimix motor running and process until the pastry is smooth and shining. Follow the choux pastry recipe on page 180.

Coconut   Process fresh coconut through the juice extractor to obtain coconut milk for curries and other recipes.

Cod's Roe   Use smoked cod's roe to make excellent taramasalata in your Magimix food processor with the metal blade (see recipe on page 55).

Cold meat   Utilize your cold cooked meat of any kind to make delicious leftover dishes in your Magimix food processor using the metal blade.

Courgettes   Slice courgettes with the slicing blade to make fritters or excellent vegetable dishes. Purée cooked courgettes to make the base of delicious summer soups.

Cream   Your Magimix food processor is so powerful that you must take care when you are whipping double cream that you do not process it for too long and thus end up with too thick a mixture.

Croûtons Place roughly broken up slices of white bread with the crusts removed in the Magimix bowl and process with the metal blade for just a few seconds until the bread is chopped to pieces roughly 2 cm ($\frac{3}{4}$ in.) in size. Fry the coarse breadcrumbs in hot dripping or lard, drain on kitchen paper and serve with soups.

Cucumber Cut the thinnest, most even slices of cucumber, with or without the peel, with the Magimix slicing disc to use in salads or summer sandwiches.

Curry Grind the spices for your curry in the Magimix food processor using the metal blade.

Dips Delicious and exciting savoury dips can be made in seconds with the Magimix metal blade. Use your imagination to create a really sensational result.

Eggs Beat egg yolks with the metal blade to form the basis of many puddings and savoury dishes. Add egg yolks through the feed tube when a recipe calls for eggs to be added one by one and beaten into a mixture.

Make your omelettes or scrambled eggs in the Magimix food processor. Be careful not to overprocess and enjoy the most perfect results.

NOTE The Magimix food processor is too fast and strong to beat egg whites stiffly but these can be beaten with a rotary or electric whisk and lightly incorporated into other ingredients which have been processed in the Magimix food processor with the metal blade. Once the beaten egg whites have been added do not process for more than 2 seconds to mix lightly.

Fats Butter and margarine for use in cakes, biscuits and other recipes can be creamed in seconds in the Magimix food processor using the metal blade.

Fennel Finely chop fennel in a clean Magimix bowl by using the metal blade to add to soups and sauces to give a light aniseed flavouring.

Fennel, florentine Slice florentine fennel with the slicing disc to add to salads for a really interesting taste and a crisp texture. Purée cooked florentine fennel with the metal blade to make a delicious base for an unusual vegetable or a good winter soup.

Fish Flake or purée raw or cooked fish in the Magimix food processor using the metal blade to form the basis of dishes as simple as fishcakes or as sophisticated as quenelles.

Flans Let your Magimix food processor help you to make the fillings for both sweet flans and savoury quiches. Use the slicing attachment and the metal blade. Make the pastry for your flans and quiches by using the metal blade and following the basic recipe on page 179.

Fruit Purée raw or cooked fruit in the Magimix bowl using the metal blade. Extract fruit juice with the juice extractor.

Game Use game to make the basis of delicious game pies, pâtés and terrines in your Magimix food processor with the metal blade.

Grapefruit Use your Magimix metal blade to help you prepare delicious marmalade, or the juice extractor to provide delicious really fresh fruit juice when these fruit are cheap and plentiful.

Grating The grating disc of your Magimix food processor will grate ingredients for any recipe.

Grinding Any ingredients that require being ground or finely minced can be processed in the Magimix food processor using the metal blade.

Hachoir Give it away! Now you have a Magimix food processor you need never chop anything by hand again.

Haddock Flake or purée cooked smoked haddock with the metal blade to make appetizing kedgeree, fishcakes, mousses and pâtés.

Ham Chop or grind ham with the metal blade to make potted dishes, risottos, salads and countless other dishes.

Hazel nuts Chop or grind hazelnuts with the metal blade to incorporate into puddings and sweets.

Herbs Chop all herbs in a clean and dry Magimix bowl using the metal blade.

Hollandaise sauce This used to be one of the difficult sauces to make but with your Magimix food processor to hand the procedure is easy (see recipe on page 157).

Ice Crush small ice cubes in your Magimix food processor using the metal blade to provide crushed ice for parties or for resting dishes on that need to be served really icy cold.

17

Ice cream Adapt any ice cream recipe and make it in your Magimix food processor taking full advantage of the strength the Magimix food processor provides for beating and mixing.

Jam Use the juice extractor to extract juice for jellies and clear jams.

Kebabs Make the marinade for your kebabs in your Magimix food processor using the metal blade and incorporating all the ingredients in the Magimix bowl.

Lamb Use tough or scrag ends of lamb to make excellent ground meat patties. Make good pâtés from minced or ground lamb's liver and utilize cooked lamb by chopping it finely with the metal blade to form the basis of any number of delicious recipes. Use top quality chopped or ground lamb for making your favourite moussaka recipe.

Leeks Process cooked leeks to make a purée, using the metal blade, for the basis of both hot and cold soups.

Lemons Use the metal blade to chop lemons for making marmalade. Use the juice extractor (peel the lemons first) to produce juice when the fruit is at its cheapest. Lemon juice can be frozen in ice cube containers and kept in the deep freeze.

Liver Finely chop or grind pig's, ox or lamb's liver to make the basis of delicious pâtés and terrines using the metal blade.

Lobster If you are lucky enough to have some lobster left over, use small amounts to chop with the metal blade and incorporate with mayonnaise for a delicious salad or lobster cocktail, or process the lobster in some softened butter until a smooth paste has been produced, season the mixture with salt, freshly ground black pepper and a pinch of mace and cayenne, chill and serve with hot toast as a first course.

Mackerel Use fresh, cooked or smoked filleted mackerel to make the base of delicious pâtés. Process the boned mackerel with the metal blade and add softened butter.

Mandarins Try substituting mandarin juice for orange juice when this fruit is in season. Peel the fruit first and use the juice extractor.

Margarine Use instead of butter and cream in the Magimix food processor using the metal blade.

Marinades Make marinades in your Magimix food processor to add flavour and to tenderize ingredients.

Marmalade Use the Magimix metal blade to chop fruit for making marmalade.

Mayonnaise Save time and achieve really first-class results by making your mayonnaise in the Magimix food processor using the metal blade. Follow the recipe on page 147. For an economy mayonnaise, make half quantities of mayonnaise with olive oil in the Magimix food processor and then add half quantities of a commercial mayonnaise to the fresh ingredients in the bowl and process for a few seconds to mix.

Meat All fresh or cooked meat can be chopped or ground in the Magimix food processor using the metal blade. Because of the strong chopping action of the blade no juices are lost during the preparation and even quite inexpensive cuts of meat can be reduced to a succulent tenderness.

Melon Make a delicious and unusual soup by cooking some sweet melon in a good stock to which some curry powder or paste has been added. Purée the melon in the Magimix food processor using the metal blade.

Milk Boiling milk can be added to ingredients through the feed tube while the machine is in action.

Mincing No more messy machines or wasted juices. Your Magimix metal blade will mince as coarsely or finely as you wish it to.

Mint Finely chop mint in the dry Magimix bowl, using the metal blade. Make mint sauce or mint butters once the mint has been finely chopped, still using the metal blade.

Mousses Light hot and cold mousses can be made with the help of your Magimix food processor to process the basic ingredients. See various recipes in this book.

Mushrooms Finely chop mushrooms in the Magimix bowl using the metal blade. Slice mushrooms by using the slicing disc.

Nuts Chop or grind nuts in the Magimix bowl, using the metal blade and processing the nuts to the fineness of texture you require. Slice almonds, brazil and hazel nuts by using the slicing attachment.

Olives Purée olives in the Magimix bowl, using the metal blade to form the basis of a delicious uncooked pâté. Chop black olives with the metal blade or slice firm stuffed olives through the slicing attachment.

Onions and shallots Coarsely or finely chop onions with the metal blade or slice them through the slicing disc. Purée cooked or raw onions with the metal blade by processing them until smooth and grate small quantities of onion through the grating attachment.

Oranges Chop oranges in the Magimix bowl with the metal blade for marmalade or skin oranges when they are cheap and plentiful and extract the juice with the help of the juice extractor.

Pancakes Make all your pancake recipes in the Magimix bowl using the metal blade. Merely put all the ingredients in the bowl and process until smooth and light. Use your favourite recipe or follow the directions for pancakes on page 196.

Parsnips Chop or slice parsnips with the help of your Magimix food processor to use as a vegetable or in soups, stews and casseroles. Purée cooked parsnips with the metal blade.

Pasta Mix the ingredients for your own fresh pasta in your Magimix food processor.

Pastry Make all pastry in your Magimix food processor for speedier, better and lighter results. Use your favourite recipe combining the flour and fats, processing them until the mixture resembles coarse breadcrumbs and then incorporating enough liquid through the feed tube (with the machine switched on) to form a firm, smooth dough which will ball up around the metal blade. There is no need to chill pastry that has been made in the Magimix food processor before rolling it out.

Peas Purée mature peas for a vegetable or soup base in the Magimix food processor using the metal blade.

Peppers Finely or coarsely chop red or green peppers (with the seeds and core removed) in your Magimix food processor using the metal blade, for garnishing salads, soups, stews and casseroles.

Pineapple Purée pineapple to make the base of puddings by using the metal blade. Extract pineapple juice by peeling fresh pineapple and processing the fruit through the juice extractor.

Pizza Make your pizza dough and your fillings in the Magimix food processor. Make the dough first, using the metal blade, and leave this to rise while you make an aromatic sauce to go on top.

Pork Mince or finely grind pork with the metal blade to make the basis of delicious pâtés and terrines. Make your own sausages or sausage meat in the Magimix food processor with the metal blade and find out what delicious results you can obtain.

Potatoes Thinly slice potatoes through the slicing blade to make countless delicious potato dishes.

Puddings Most puddings require considerable and often lengthy preparation. This can usually be cut down by processing the ingredients in the Magimix food processor. See the chapter on puddings or adapt your favourite recipes.

Puréeing Nearly anything that requires puréeing can be processed in the Magimix food processor by using the metal blade and the Magimix food processor will not reduce ingredients to such a bland consistency that they lose both flavour and every particle of their texture.

Red cabbage Shred red cabbage through the slicing blade for pickling, cooking or using fresh in salads.

Rhubarb Purée cooked rhubarb in the Magimix food processor using the metal blade.

Risotto Chop the ingredients for a risotto in the Magimix food processor.

Sage Finely chop sage in a clean Magimix bowl with the metal blade to add to savoury dishes, sauces and jellies.

Salad vegetables Chop, slice or grate vegetables for salads using the metal blade, slicing disc or grating disc.

Sandwiches Make delicious sandwich fillings in your Magimix food processor. See pages 173–76 for recipes.

Sauces Most of the classic sauces take time to make. Your Magimix food processor can help by finely chopping ingredients and mixing or beating. Boiling liquids can be incorporated into other ingredients by pouring them through the feed tube while the machine is switched on.

Sausages Make your own sausages with pork, beef or lamb in the Magimix food processor by finely chopping or grinding the ingredients with the metal blade. See recipes on pages 101–2.

Slicing Your slicing attachment will produce even slices in seconds.

Sorbets Fruit juice for sorbets can be produced in the juice and vegetable extractor.

Soufflés Incredibly light soufflés can be produced in your Magimix food processor. Combine all the ingredients except the egg white and process in the Magimix food processor using the metal blade. Whip egg whites until stiff and lightly fold into the basic ingredients before turning into a soufflé dish.

Soups Use your Magimix food processor to chop, grate or purée ingredients for almost any soup.

Spaghetti Make delicious sauces in only minutes with the aid of your Magimix food processor and the metal blade.

Spinach Extract health giving spinach juice using the fruit and vegetable juice extractor. Finely chop or purée spinach in the Magimix bowl using the metal blade.

Sponge cakes Cream the butter and sugar for your sponge in the Magimix food processor using the metal blade. Add the eggs through the feed tube with the machine switched on. Whip the egg whites until stiff and put them in the bowl with the other ingredients. Process for 2 seconds and cook as usual.

Steak Make the perfect steak tartare or steak hamburger by processing the meat, with all gristle removed, in the Magimix food processor using the metal blade.

Stuffings Prepare breadcrumbs and make stuffings with grated or chopped ingredients in only a few minutes in your Magimix food processor.

Suet Suet can be grated or finely chopped in the Magimix food processor for use in all recipes that call for suet in the ingredients.

Tarragon Finely chop tarragon in a clean, dry Magimix bowl, using the metal blade.

Thyme   Finely chop thyme in a clean, dry Magimix bowl, using the metal blade.

Tomatoes   Some of the best dishes in the world call for tomatoes in their ingredients. Chopped or puréed tomatoes can all be prepared in your Magimix food processor with the metal blade; tomato sauces are better than ever before if you make them in the Magimix processor and even tomato recipes like a topping for pizza, tomato soups and sauces can all be made to perfection in your Magimix food processor. Tomato juice from fresh tomatoes can be made in your Magimix juice extractor attachment.

Tongue   Exciting dishes can be made from chopped or sliced tongue – just let the Magimix food processor do the work for you. Chop tongue very finely with the metal blade to make delicious first courses or sandwich fillings with a potted recipe (see page 44).

Turkey   Don't sigh over your leftover turkey after Christmas day any more. With your Magimix food processor you can make countless delicious dishes from the leftovers, using the cooked poultry to its best advantage.

Turnips   Turnips are sometimes considered rather a poor man's vegetable, but finely chopped in your Magimix food processor they make a good addition to mixed vegetable soups, a good puréed vegetable and, grated, they also make a delicious addition to winter salads.

Vegetables   All vegetables can be chopped, puréed or grated with the help of your Magimix food processor. Whenever you read a recipe that calls for the preparation of a vegetable check and see whether the Magimix food processor can help you with its preparation – the answer will almost certainly be 'yes'.

Walnuts   Chop fresh or roasted walnuts in your Magimix bowl with a metal blade to add to both sweet and savoury dishes.

Watercress   Autumn soups based on potatoes and watercress are always popular. You can purée the vegetables in your Magimix bowl using the metal blade. Very finely chopped watercress can also be a good garnish or make a delicious salad ingredient. Chop the watercress in a clean, dry Magimix bowl, using the metal blade.

Water ices   Prepare the fruit juice for water ices by using the Magimix fruit and vegetable extractor. Water ices can

23

be based on the juice of almost any fruit in season (see recipes on page 208).

White sauce Even the best cooks find that their white sauce sometimes curdles or goes lumpy. If this happens

Soups

Avocado soup

Serves 4

A pale green, chilled soup that makes a delicious starter for a summer meal. The soup is rather on the rich side so serve it before a light main course.

1 large ripe avocado
1 spring onion
2 sprigs fresh dill or a
*   small bunch chives*
1 teaspoon lemon juice
9 dl (1½ pints) chicken
*   stock*

3 dl (½ pint) single cream
salt and freshly ground
*   black pepper*
4 slices of lemon

USE THE
METAL BLADE

Peel the avocado and cut into four pieces. Roughly chop the spring onion. Roughly chop the chives.

Place the dill or chives in the Magimix bowl and process until the herbs are finely chopped. Remove the herbs. Put the avocado, lemon juice and spring onion in the Magimix bowl and process until smooth. With the machine running, gradually add as much stock as the bowl will take. Pour into a bowl, add the remaining stock, mix in the cream and season with salt and freshly ground black pepper. Mix in the herbs and chill until really cold before serving.

Serve with a thin slice of lemon floating on each bowl.

Cold cucumber soup

Serves 4

1 cucumber
6 spring onion tops
2 medium potatoes
25 g (1 oz) butter
9 dl (1½ pints) white stock

salt and white pepper
4 tablespoons double cream
a few tarragon or mint
* leaves*

Slice the cucumber without peeling it. Remove the cucumber.

USE THE SLICING DISC

USE THE METAL BLADE

Process the spring onion tops for a few seconds until chopped. Remove them from the bowl. Peel the potatoes and chop them into rough pieces. Process in the Magimix food processor until chopped to the size of peas.

Melt the butter in a saucepan, add the cucumber, spring onions and potatoes and cook over a low heat, stirring gently, until the butter has been absorbed. Add the stock, season well and bring to the boil. Simmer gently for about 25 minutes until the vegetables are very soft. Drain the liquid from the soup. Process the vegetables in the Magimix food processor until smooth. Return puréed vegetables to the liquid and add the cream. Slice the tarragon or mint leaves into very thin shreds with a sharp knife or scissors and stir into the soup. Chill in a refrigerator until the soup is very cold before serving.

Potato soup

Serves 4

2 leeks
37 g (1½ oz) butter
450 g (1 lb) potatoes
9 dl (1½ pints) chicken
* stock (or water and 2*
* stock cubes)*

salt and freshly ground
* black pepper*
2 sprigs parsley, stalks
* removed*
1.5 dl (¼ pint) single cream

.USE THE METAL BLADE

Chop the leeks into slices about 2.5 cm (1 in.) long and wash thoroughly.

Put the sliced leeks into the Magimix bowl and process for a few seconds until finely chopped. Melt the butter in a large pan, add the leeks and cook over a low heat until soft and transparent. Peel and roughly chop the potatoes. Place the potatoes in the Magimix bowl and process until finely chopped. Add the potatoes to the leeks and cook over a low heat for 3 minutes. Pour over the stock, season well with salt and freshly ground black pepper, add the parsley and bring the soup to the boil. Simmer gently for 20 minutes until the vegetables are just tender.

Drain off the stock and process the vegetables until smooth. Combine the stock and vegetable purée in a clean pan, blend in the cream, check seasoning and heat through without boiling.

Rich mushroom soup

Serves 6–8

2 sprigs parsley with
  stalks removed
2 onions
62 g (2½ oz) butter
37 g (1½ oz) flour
1.5 l (2¼ pints) chicken
  stock
350 g (¾ lb) firm button
  mushrooms

salt
1 teaspoon lemon juice
2 egg yolks
1.5 dl (¼ pint) single
  cream
freshly ground black
  pepper

USE THE
METAL BLADE

Process the parsley leaves until finely chopped. Remove the leaves from the bowl.

Peel and quarter the onions. Process the onions until finely chopped. Melt 37 g (1½ oz) butter in a large pan and cook the onions until soft and transparent. Stir in the flour and cook over a low heat for a few minutes, stirring continually. Gradually add the stock, mixing well until the soup is smooth.

Wipe the mushrooms with a damp cloth and remove the stems. Process the mushroom stems in the Magimix food processor until finely chopped. Stir the chopped stems into the soup, return to the heat and bring to a simmer. Partially cover the pan and simmer for about 25 minutes, skimming now and then as necessary. Strain the soup and return to the pan.

USE THE
SLICING DISC

Slice the mushroom caps through the slicing disc. In a separate pan melt 25 g (1 oz) butter, add the mushroom caps, a good pinch of salt and the lemon juice. Cover the pan and cook over a low heat for 5 minutes.

Pour the mushroom caps and juices into the soup and simmer for 10 minutes. Beat the egg yolks and cream in a large bowl. Add the hot soup very slowly, stirring well all the time. Taste for seasoning, return the soup to the sauce-pan and stir over a low heat for a few minutes until hot through but not boiling. Sprinkle some parsley over the soup before serving.

Spinach soup

Serves 4–6

Serve this soup with a garnish of chopped hard-boiled eggs and some crisply fried croûtons of bread (see page 38).

675 g (1½ lb) fresh spinach or 450 g (1 lb) frozen spinach
100 g (4 oz) butter
1 hard-boiled egg
1½ tablespoons flour
3 dl (½ pint) chicken stock

6 dl (1 pint) milk
2 teaspoons lemon juice
salt and freshly ground black pepper
Pinch grated nutmeg
3 tablespoons double cream

Remove any coarse stems from the fresh spinach and wash the leaves in plenty of cold, salted water. Drain well. Melt 50 g (2 oz) butter in a large heavy pan, add the fresh or frozen spinach and cook over a low heat, stirring to prevent sticking, until the spinach is tender.

USE THE
METAL BLADE

Quarter the hard-boiled egg, place it in the Magimix bowl and process until finely chopped. Remove the egg and set on one side.

Place the spinach in the Magimix bowl and process until puréed. Melt the remaining butter in a saucepan, add the flour and mix well. Gradually blend in the stock and milk, stirring continually over a medium high heat until the sauce comes to the boil and is thick and smooth. Add the lemon juice and mix in the spinach purée (if the soup is too thick, thin it with a little extra stock). Season with salt and freshly ground black pepper and a pinch of nutmeg and simmer for 5 minutes. Stir in the cream and heat through without boiling. Serve the soup with a scattering of chopped hard-boiled egg in each bowl and a bowl of crisply fried bread croûtons on the side.

Sorrel and potato soup

Serves 6

A creamy, subtly flavoured soup that has a real country air about it. Sorrel can be picked from the hedgerows where it grows wild or it can be cultivated with the greatest possible ease in the garden. Cultivated sorrel has a slightly less bitter-sweet flavour than wild sorrel.

175 g (6 oz) sorrel leaves
350 g (12 oz) potatoes
37 g (1½ oz) butter
1.5 l (2¼ pints) chicken or
* white stock*
salt and freshly ground
* black pepper*
2 egg yolks
4 tablespoons single
* cream or creamy milk*

Peel and quarter the shallot. Wash the sorrel, cut out any tough stalks and roughly shred the leaves. Peel and roughly chop the potatoes.

USE THE
METAL BLADE

Place the shallot in the Magimix bowl and process until finely chopped. Remove the shallot, place the potatoes in the bowl and process until the potatoes are roughly chopped and about the size of large peas.

Melt the butter in a saucepan. Add the shallot and cook over a low heat until the shallot is soft and transparent. Add the sorrel and cook for a further 2 minutes until the sorrel is soft. Add the potatoes, mix well and pour on the stock. Bring to the boil, season with salt and pepper and simmer for about 30 minutes until the potatoes are very soft. Remove from the heat and drain off the liquid from the pan.

Place the vegetables in the Magimix bowl and process until smooth. Return to a clean pan, blend in the cooking liquid, egg yolks and cream, heat through without boiling, check seasoning and serve with fried croûtons of bread (see page 38).

31

Potage Crécy

Serves 4–6

225 g (8 oz) onions
675 g (1½ lb) carrots
450 g (1 lb) potatoes
75 g (3 oz) butter
1.2 l (2 pints) chicken
stock or water

salt and freshly ground
black pepper
1 teaspoon sugar
1 sprig thyme
4 sprigs parsley or chervil
fried bread croûtons (see
page 38)

Peel and halve the onions. Peel the carrots, peel and quarter the potatoes.

USE THE
SLICING DISC

Slice the onions through the slicing blade and remove from the bowl. Slice the carrots through the slicing blade and remove from the bowl. Slice the potatoes through the slicing blade and remove from the bowl.

Melt the butter in a heavy pan. Add the onions, potatoes and carrots and cook over a low heat for 20 minutes, stirring to prevent sticking until the butter has all been absorbed and the vegetables are soft. Add the stock, season with salt and plenty of freshly ground black pepper, add the sugar and thyme and bring to the boil. Cover and cook over a low heat for 15–20 minutes until the vegetables are very soft. Strain off the liquid and remove the thyme.

USE THE
METAL BLADE

Put the vegetables in the Magimix bowl and process until smooth. Return to a clean pan with the stock, check seasoning and heat through.

Wash and dry the Magimix bowl and metal blade. Place the parsley or chervil leaves in the Magimix bowl and process until finely chopped.

Mix the chopped herbs into the soup before serving. Hand fried croûtons round on the side.

Celery soup

Serves 4

450 g (1 lb) celery stalks
(outside stalks are ideal)
1 onion
37 g (1½ oz) butter
3 dl (½ pint) white stock

6 dl (1 pint) milk
salt and freshly ground
black pepper
lemon juice

USE THE
SLICING DISC

Wash the celery and slice the stalks through the slicing disc. Remove the celery.

Peel and quarter the onion and process until finely chopped. Melt the butter in a large heavy pan and add the vegetables. Put the lid on the pan and cook over a gentle heat for 10 minutes shaking now and then to prevent sticking.

Pour in the stock and the milk, season with salt and freshly ground black pepper, bring to the boil and simmer gently for about 30 minutes until the celery is soft. Strain the soup, reserve the stock and purée the vegetables in the Magimix food processor until smooth. Combine the stock and purée in a clean pan and heat through.

Check for seasoning and add lemon juice to taste.

Cream of broad bean soup

Serves 4

6 sprigs parsley
2 onions
4 sage leaves or pinch
  dried sage
25 g (1 oz) butter
9 dl (1½ pints) milk

450 g (1 lb) shelled broad
  beans
salt and freshly ground
  black pepper
4 tablespoons double cream

Remove the stalks from two of the parsley sprigs and process the leaves in the Magimix bowl until finely chopped. Remove the parsley. Peel and quarter the onions. Place the onions and sage leaves in the Magimix bowl and process until the onions are finely chopped. Melt the butter in a saucepan and cook the onion and sage over a low heat until the onion is soft and transparent. Pour in the milk and add the four remaining parsley sprigs, the broad beans, dried sage (if you used it), salt and plenty of freshly ground black pepper. Cook over a low heat for about 45 minutes or until the beans are tender.

Drain off the liquid, remove the parsley sprigs and process the vegetables in the Magimix food processor until they are reduced to a smooth purée. Combine the purée and liquid in a clean pan, mix well and heat through.

Put a tablespoon of cream into each of four warm soup bowls, pour in the soup and sprinkle each bowl with a little of the chopped parsley.

Bacon and cabbage soup with Brie

Serves 6

Some of the greatest satisfaction in cooking often comes from producing something gloriously simple and inexpensive that, in its own way, tastes as delicious and satisfying as the most rich and complicated of dishes. Many of the soups I make at Maidenwell, my home in Cornwall, come into this category. There I have access to the best of all ingredients, vegetables from the garden, eaten within hours of being dug up, and with these and my Magimix food processor I produce soups that, in their simplicity and purity, delight both my family and friends. In this recipe small squares of Brie in the bottom of the soup bowls add an extra, luxurious touch.

100 g (4 oz) streaky bacon	1.5 l (2½ pints) chicken
1 onion	stock
350 g (¾ lb) potatoes	pinch dried summer savory
1 small Savoy cabbage	salt and freshly ground
1 tablespoon olive or	black pepper
vegetable oil	100 g (4 oz) Brie cheese

Remove the rind from the bacon and roughly chop the rashers. Peel and roughly chop the onion. Peel and roughly chop the potatoes. Remove the outer leaves and the tough core of the cabbage.

USE THE
METAL BLADE

Place the bacon and onion in the Magimix bowl and process until the ingredients are finely chopped.

Heat the oil in a large, heavy saucepan. Add the bacon and onion and cook over a low heat until the onion is soft and transparent.

Place the potatoes in the Magimix bowl and process until the potatoes are chopped to about the size of peas.

Add the potatoes to the saucepan and continue to cook over a low heat until all the oil and fat has been absorbed by the ingredients.

USE THE
SLICING DISC

Shred the cabbage through the slicing disc. Add the cabbage to the ingredients in the pan, mix well, add the stock, bring to the boil and add the savory and season with salt and pepper. Cover the pan and simmer the soup for about 20 minutes until the potatoes are tender.

Thinly cut off the rind from the Brie and cut the cheese into 1 cm (½ in.) squares. Place the cheese in the bottom of six warmed soup bowls and pour over the hot soup.

Serve at once.

Parsnip soup à l'oignon

Serves 4

1 large parsnip
1 onion
75 g (3 oz) butter
1 clove garlic, crushed
1 tablespoon flour
1 teaspoon curry powder

1.2 l (2 pints) hot beef
   stock
salt and freshly ground
   black pepper
1.5 dl ($\frac{1}{4}$ pint) cream or
   top of the milk

Peel and quarter the parsnip and onion.

USE THE
SLICING DISC

Slice the parsnip and onion through the slicing disc. Melt the butter in a large, heavy pan and add the sliced parsnip and onion and the crushed garlic clove. Mix well to coat the vegetables with butter, put a lid on the pan and cook over a very low heat for 10 minutes, shaking the pan now and then. Sprinkle over the flour and curry powder and mix well. Gradually blend in the hot stock, stirring continually, and bring to the boil. Simmer the soup for 20 minutes until the vegetables are soft.

USE THE
METAL BLADE

Strain the soup, place the vegetables in the Magimix bowl and process until reduced to a smooth purée. Return the vegetables to a clean saucepan, mix in the liquid, season with salt and freshly ground black pepper, stir in the cream and heat through without boiling.
Serve the soup with croûtons of crisply fried bread.

Carrot and celery soup

Serves 4

Chopping and slicing the vegetables enables this soup to cook in a surprisingly short time. Make it at the end of the winter when old carrots are still around and celery is plentiful.
Serve it with crisp croûtons of fried bread.

225 g ($\frac{1}{2}$ lb) carrots
4 sticks celery
1 onion
1 medium potato
50 g (2 oz) butter

9 dl (1$\frac{1}{2}$ pints) chicken
   stock (or water and
   stock cube)
celery salt and freshly
   ground black pepper

Peel the carrots. Wash the celery stalks and trim off the leaves. Peel and halve the onion. Peel and roughly chop the potato.

Place the celery leaves in the Magimix bowl and process until the leaves are finely chopped. Remove the leaves and reserve for garnishing this soup. Place the potatoes in the Magimix bowl and process until chopped to the size of peas. Remove the potatoes.

Slice the carrot, onion and celery through the slicing disc.

Melt the butter in a large saucepan. Add the vegetables and cook over a low heat, stirring every now and then until the butter is absorbed into the vegetables. Add the stock, mix well, season with celery salt and freshly ground black pepper, bring to the boil and simmer for about 15 minutes until the vegetables are tender. Strain off the liquid from the soup and purée the vegetables in the Magimix food processor until smooth.

Combine the vegetable purée and liquid in a clean pan, heat through and add the celery leaves just before serving.

Winter velvet

Serves 4

A soup of combined leeks and parsnips with a creamy colour and texture. Garnish with croûtons of crisply fried bread or with chopped parsley.

350 g ($\frac{3}{4}$ lb) parsnips	*1.2 l (2 pints) stock*
225 (8 oz) leeks	*salt, pepper and $\frac{1}{4}$*
1 medium potato	*teaspoon grated nutmeg*
1 small onion	*1.5 dl ($\frac{1}{4}$ pint) single cream*

Peel the parsnips. Wash and trim the leeks. Peel the potato. Peel the onion.

Slice the parsnips, leeks, potato and onion through the slicing disc. Place the vegetables in a heavy saucepan and pour over the stock. Season with salt, pepper and nutmeg, bring to the boil and simmer for 20 minutes or until the vegetables are tender. Strain off the stock.

Place the strained vegetables in the Magimix bowl and process until they are reduced to a smooth purée. Return the purée to a clean saucepan, add the stock and mix well. Heat through, check seasoning and stir in the cream before serving.

Carrot, tomato and orange soup

Serves 4

leaves of 2 celery stalks
450 g (1 lb) carrots
2 medium onions
37 g (1½ oz) butter
2 tablespoons home-made
*   tomato purée (see*
*   page 162)*

1 l (1¾ pints) stock
salt and freshly ground
*   black pepper*
juice of 1½ oranges
thinly pared rind of 1
*   orange*
4 tablespoons double cream

Peel the carrots and onions.

USE THE
METAL BLADE

Place the celery leaves in the Magimix bowl and process until the leaves are finely chopped. Remove the leaves and set aside for garnishing.

USE THE
SLICING DISC

Slice the carrots and onions through the slicing disc.

Melt the butter in a large saucepan. Add the carrots and onions and cook over a low heat, stirring to prevent sticking, for 5 minutes. Add the tomato purée, mix well and gradually blend in the stock. Bring to the boil and simmer for about 20 minutes or until the vegetables are absolutely tender.

Drain off the stock, place the vegetables in the Magimix bowl and process until they are reduced to a smooth purée.

Return the purée to a clean pan, add the stock, mix well and reheat. Season with salt and freshly ground black pepper and mix in the orange juice.

Cut the orange rind into very thin strips and blanch in boiling water for 5 minutes. Drain well.

Pour the soup into heated serving bowls and float the cream over the top. Sprinkle the cream with the orange rind and celery leaves and serve at once.

Bread bits to serve with soup or game

Serves 4

I used to spend hours either chopping up bread into neat little cubes for various soups or grating white bread to fry and serve with roast game. Now I merely cut the crusts off some slices of white bread, process them in the Magimix and cut that particular chore by half the time.

2 thick cut slices white
bread

3 tablespoons olive oil or
37 g (1½ oz) lard

USE THE
METAL BLADE

Remove the crusts from the slices of bread and roughly tear up the slices. Place the bread in the Magimix bowl and process for exactly 5 seconds until the bread is chopped to the size of small peas.

Heat the oil or lard in a frying pan, add the bread and cook over a medium heat, stirring occasionally, until the pieces of bread are crisp and golden brown. Drain on kitchen paper.

Serve in a bowl with roast game or sprinkle over the top of vegetable soup.

Starters and hors d'oeuvres

Notes on cooking pâtés and terrines etc

A pâté is a smooth textured combination of lean and fat meat or fish, well flavoured and seasoned and usually cooked in a bain marie. Pâtés can also be made from cooked ingredients and they may have spinach or sorrel added for taste and colouring. A terrine is a coarsely textured variation of a pâté.

Pâtés and terrines should never be overcooked and the colour of a meat pâté or terrine should be pink rather than grey. To check whether a pâté or terrine is cooked, either plunge a knitting needle into the pâté and if it comes out clean the pâté is done, or check whether the pâté has shrunk away from the sides of the dish in which case it will also be done.

To check seasoning when making a pâté, fry a spoonful of the mixture in a little butter over a high heat and taste to test. Cooked pâtés and terrines usually need to be weighted in order to consolidate the ingredients after they have been removed from the oven. The best way to do this is to cut a piece of hardboard just a fraction smaller than the terrine, cover it with foil, place it over the cooked ingredients and press down with a heavy

39

weight (I usually use a large tin of fruit). Chill the weighted pâté for at least 6 hours before turning out. Both pâtés and terrines benefit by being left overnight to allow the flavours to mature.

BRAWN

This is an English dish made from boiled meats covered in their own jellied stock and chilled in a mould. Usually brawn is made from highly gelatinous ingredients such as the heads or feet of animals.

GALANTINES

Galantines are usually made from white meat with the addition of ham and other ingredients, cooked in the skin of a boned bird, weighted and served cold cut into thin slices.

MEAT LOAVES

Minced meat is bound with beaten egg, well flavoured and served either hot with a sauce or cold. Flavouring and seasoning is very important or a meat loaf is inclined to be tasteless.

POTTED MEATS, POULTRY AND FISH

Meat, poultry or fish reduced to a smooth consistency or shredded are combined with melted or clarified butter and chilled to make a paste. Potted ingredients can be eaten with toast or used as a sandwich filling.

Game pâté

Serves 10

2 cloves garlic
4 juniper berries
1 egg
pinch mace
¼ teaspoon mixed sage
  and thyme
salt and freshly ground
  black pepper
2 bay leaves

450 g (1 lb) lean veal
2 tablespoons brandy
2 tablespoons dry white
  wine
1 pheasant (or wild duck,
  2 partridges or 3
  pigeons)
25 g (1 oz) butter
450 g (1 lb) fat pork

USE THE
METAL BLADE

Trim the veal and cut into 2.5 cm (1 in.) cubes. Combine the brandy and wine, add the veal and leave to marinate for 1 hour. Drain and reserve the marinade.

Rub the pheasant or other game, inside and outside, with the butter and half roast in a hot oven (200°C, 400°F. Reg. 6) for 20–30 minutes. Leave to cool, reserve the juices in the pan, remove the flesh from the bones (the carcass can be used for soup). Discard any skin or sinews from the flesh.

Remove any rind from the pork and cut half the meat into 2.5 cm (1 in.) cubes. Cut the remaining fat into thin matchstick strips.

Peel the garlic and crush the juniper berries with the back of a fork.

Place half the veal in the Magimix bowl and process until the ingredients are very finely ground. Remove and process the rest of the veal to the same consistency. Remove the veal and process the cubed pork in the same way. Remove the pork and place the pheasant or other game meat in the Magimix bowl with the egg, mace, garlic, juniper berries, sage and thyme and season generously with salt and freshly ground black pepper. Process until the game is very finely ground and the ingredients are well mixed.

Combine all the ingredients in a bowl with the juices from the roasting tin and the remaining marinade and mix well.

Line a terrine with half the strips of pork fat. Pack the pâté into the terrine and press down firmly. Top with remaining strips of pork fat and with the bay leaves. Cover with a double layer of buttered foil, stand in a roasting tin filled with enough hot water to come half way up the sides of the terrine and cook in a slow oven

41

(130°C, 250°F, Reg. 1) for $2\frac{1}{2}$ hours. The pâté is cooked when it shrinks away from the sides of the terrine.

Cover with a weight and leave to stand until cool. Chill in a refrigerator for at least 24 hours before turning out.

Pork and herb terrine

Serves 6

This is a simple French country style terrine that makes a good picnic dish for hot summer days. You can also serve the terrine hot on a winter's day with jacket potatoes and a green salad.

*2 tablespoons mixed
  parsley, basil, savory
  and rosemary leaves
1 onion
1 clove garlic
100 g (4 oz) cooked ham
100 g (4 oz) streaky bacon
450 g (1 lb) fat pork (belly
  is good for this providing
  the ratio of fat is fairly high)*

*1 egg
450 g (1 lb) spinach
freshly ground black pepper
225 g (8 oz) very fat bacon
  or pork fat cut into thin
  slices
1 small bay leaf*

USE THE
METAL BLADE

Remove the stalks from the herbs and place the herbs in the Magimix bowl. Process until the herbs are finely chopped. Remove the herbs and put them into a large bowl.

Peel and roughly chop the onion and garlic. Roughly chop the ham. Remove the rind from the bacon and fat pork and roughly chop the flesh.

Combine the ham and bacon in the Magimix bowl and process until the ham and bacon are finely chopped. Remove and add the ham and bacon to the chopped herbs. Place the onion and garlic in the bowl with half of the fat pork and process until the meat is finely ground. Remove and add to the bacon and ham. Place the remaining fat pork in the Magimix bowl and process until the meat is finely ground. Break the egg into the bowl and continue to process until the egg is mixed with the pork. Remove and add to the rest of the meat.

Wash the spinach and cook it over a high heat without extra water until just tender (about 4 minutes). Drain really well.

42

Place the spinach in the Magimix bowl and process until chopped (do not over process). Add the spinach to the other ingredients, season with freshly ground black pepper and mix well.

Line a 1.2 l (2 pint) terrine with slices of fat bacon or pork fat (remove the rind if necessary). Pack in the terrine mixture and top with remaining slices of fat bacon or pork fat. Top with the bay leaf, cover tightly with foil and stand in a baking tin with hot water coming half way up the side of the terrine. Cook in a preheated very moderate oven (170°C, 325°F, Reg. 3) for 1 hour or until the sides of the terrine have shrunk from the sides of the dish.

Potted beef

Serves 4 as a first course

A traditional British 'classic' that makes a good first course as an alternative to a pâté or terrine to serve with hot toast or which can be used as a very superior sandwich filling. To make this dish by hand requires a long period of pounding but with the Magimix food processor the right texture is produced with no trouble at all.

450 g (1 lb) topside beef
beef stock ·
bouquet garni
salt and freshly ground
*   black pepper*
1 small clove garlic

½ teaspoon mace
pinch ground nutmeg
50 g (2 oz) butter
1 anchovy fillet
1 tablespoon port

Place the meat in a roasting tin and roast in a hot oven (220°C, 425°F, Reg. 7) for 20 minutes. Reserve any meat juice in the pan, transfer the meat to a baking dish, pour over enough stock to cover, add the bouquet garni and season with salt and freshly ground black pepper. Cover tightly with foil and bake in a slow oven (150°C, 300°F, Reg. 2) for 2–2½ hours until the meat is tender. Leave to cool in the stock and then drain and remove the bouquet garni (the stock can be used as a deliciously flavoured base for soups, sauces or gravies).

Cut the meat into 2.5 cm (1 in.) cubes. Peel the garlic.

USE THE
METAL BLADE

Place the meat and garlic in the Magimix bowl. Season with the mace and nutmeg and add the butter and anchovy. Process until the meat is reduced to a coarse paste. With

43

the machine switched on, add the port through the feed tube. Check for seasoning, pack in an earthenware pot and chill for at least an hour before serving. The meat can be covered with a layer of clarified butter and kept for up to two weeks in a refrigerator.

Potted tongue

This can be served as a first course with hot toast or used as a sandwich spread.

340 g (12 oz) cooked
   tongue
pinch cayenne pepper,
   allspice and ground
   mace

salt and freshly ground
   black pepper
2 tablespoons red wine
170 g (6 oz) softened butter

Roughly chop the tongue.

USE THE
METAL BLADE

Place the tongue in the Magimix bowl with the seasonings and process until the ingredients are reduced to a fine paste. Add the red wine and continue to process until the wine is absorbed. Add 100 g (4 oz) of the butter cut into pieces and process until the mixture is smooth. Check seasoning and pack into small pots.

Heat the remaining butter until foaming and pour it over the top of the pots through a sieve lined with muslin. Chill before serving.

Note: The same recipe can be used for making potted ham, a mixture of half ham and half cooked game, cooked turkey or cooked salmon.

Pheasant pâté with olives

Serves 8

This is also good made with wild duck or a couple of partridges. The olives lighten the texture and add colour to the pâté.

1 young pheasant
4 tablespoons brandy
225 g (8 oz) pie veal
225 g (8 oz) fat belly pork
1 shallot
1 teaspoon parsley leaves
¼ teaspoon sage and thyme
*   leaves*

1 large egg
50 g (2 oz) green olives
*   with the stones removed*
salt and freshly ground
*   black pepper*
225 g (8 oz) very fat bacon
*   rashers or thin slices of*
*   pork fat*

Remove the skin from the pheasant and cut off the breast meat. Cut the breasts into very thin slices. Pour over the brandy and leave to marinate for 2 hours.

Cut off the rest of the meat from the pheasant and chop it roughly discarding any tough tendons. Roughly chop the veal, remove the skin from the belly pork and roughly chop the meat. Peel and quarter the shallot.

USE THE
METAL BLADE

Remove any stalks from the herbs, place the herbs in the Magimix bowl and process until finely chopped. Add the chopped pheasant and continue to process until the meat is the consistency of coarsely minced meat. Remove the pheasant to a large bowl and place the veal in the Magimix bowl. Process until the veal is finely chopped and add it to the pheasant. Place the pork belly in the bowl with the shallot and process until the belly is the consistency of sausage meat. Add the egg, half the olives and the brandy marinade and continue to process until the ingredients are well mixed. Add to the other ingredients except the pheasant breasts, season and mix well.

Line a 9 dl (1½ pint) terrine with rashers of bacon or slices of pork fat, derinded, and fill with half the mixed ingredients. Top with the pheasant breasts and remaining olives, halved, and cover with the rest of the mixed ingredients. Top with the remaining bacon slices or slices of pork fat and cover the terrine tightly with foil. Set the terrine in a baking tin, pour enough hot water in the tin to come half way up the sides and cook in the centre of a very moderate oven (170°C, 325°F, Reg. 3) for 1¼ hours.

Remove from the baking tin, weight down and leave to cool. Chill until really cold and turn out to serve with hot toast or French bread.

Turkey pâté

Serves 6

If you have problems coping with all that leftover turkey after Christmas try this simple pâté. It makes a good light meal after all that rich food.

1 onion
25 g (1 oz) butter
275–350 g (10–12 oz)
*   cooked turkey meat*
225 g (8 oz) fat belly of
*   pork*
100 g (4 oz) bread with the
*   crusts removed*
milk

30 ml (2 tablespoons)
*   Béchamel sauce*
1 egg
pinch mixed dried herbs
pinch mixed spice
½ teaspoon Worcestershire
*   sauce*
salt and freshly ground
*   black pepper*

USE THE
METAL BLADE

Peel and quarter the onion.

Fry the onion in the butter over a low heat until soft and transparent. Roughly chop the turkey. Remove the rind from the pork belly and roughly chop the meat. Soak the bread in a little milk until soft and squeeze out excess milk.

Place the belly pork in the Magimix bowl and process until it is the consistency of sausage meat. Add the turkey meat, onion, bread, sauce and egg and process until the turkey is very finely chopped. Add the herbs, spice and Worcestershire sauce, season with salt and freshly ground black pepper and switch the machine on and off to mix the ingredients.

Well butter a 9 dl (1½ pint) terrine, spoon in the terrine mixture, packing it down firmly with the back of a wooden spoon, and cover it tightly with well buttered foil. Place the terrine in a baking tin, pour in enough hot water to come half way up the sides of the terrine and cook in a pre-heated very moderate oven (170°C, 325°F, Reg. 3) for 1¼ hours. Remove from the baking tin, cool and then chill in a refrigerator until set firm.

Serve cold with hot French bread and a green or mixed salad.

Pâté de la forêt

A highly seasoned pâté of pigeons' breasts flavoured with brandy and anchovy fillets.

175 g (6 oz) calf's liver	*4 juniper berries, crushed*
225 g (8 oz) pork belly	*3 anchovies*
breasts of 3 pigeons	*1 tablespoon brandy*
1 bunch chervil	*freshly ground black pepper*
1 small onion	*4 rashers streaky bacon*
2 cloves garlic	*2 bay leaves*
50 g (2 oz) butter	

Cut the liver into 2.5 cm (1 in.) cubes. Cut the pork belly into 2.5 cm (1 in.) cubes. Cut the pigeon breasts into very thin strips. Remove the tough stalks from the chervil. Peel and roughly chop the onion. Peel and roughly chop the garlic. Melt the butter and leave to cool.

USE THE
METAL BLADE

Place the chervil leaves in the Magimix bowl and process until the leaves are finely chopped. Add the onion, garlic, juniper berries and anchovies to the chervil and process until the onion is finely chopped. Add the liver to the ingredients in the Magimix bowl and process until the liver is reduced to a purée. Remove the ingredients from the Magimix bowl and place them in a mixing bowl. Place the pork belly in the Magimix bowl and process until the belly is reduced to a smooth purée. Add the brandy and butter, season with freshly ground black pepper and process until the ingredients are well mixed. Combine the ingredients from the Magimix bowl with the mixture in the mixing bowl and mix well. Remove the rinds from the bacon rashers and stretch the rashers by running the back of a knife over them. Place two of the rashers in the bottom of a terrine and pack half of the pâté firmly on top of the bacon. Cover with the thin strips of pigeons' breasts, put the remaining pâté on next and top with the remaining rashers of bacon and with the bay leaves. Cover the terrine tightly with foil.

Stand the terrine in a baking tin and pour in enough hot water to come half way up the sides of the terrine. Bake in a moderate oven (180°C, 350°F, Reg. 4) for 1 hour or until the sides of the pâté are coming cleanly away from the sides of the terrine.

Weight down, cool and chill for at least 6 hours before slicing and serving with hot toast or French bread.

Terrine maison

Serves 8–10

A coarse textured pâté of veal, liver and bacon. Very finely chop the ingredients without puréeing them.

100 g (4 oz) fat bacon
175 g (6 oz) calf's liver
350 g (12 oz) pie veal
1 onion
small bunch of parsley or chervil
2 cloves garlic
6 thin rashers streaky bacon
75 g (3 oz) butter

4 sage leaves (or $\frac{1}{4}$ teaspoon dried sage)
$\frac{1}{4}$ teaspoon oregano
pinch mace
salt and freshly ground black pepper
1 egg
2 tablespoons double cream
90 ml (3 fl. oz) red wine
3 bay leaves

Roughly chop the fat bacon. Cut the liver into 2.5 cm (1 in.) pieces. Cut the pie veal into 2.5 cm (1 in.) cubes. Peel and roughly chop the onion. Remove the tough stalks of the parsley or chervil. Peel the garlic cloves. Remove the rinds from the bacon rashers and stretch the rashers by running the back of a knife along them. Melt the butter and leave to cool.

USE THE
METAL BLADE

Combine the sage, parsley or chervil leaves and the oregano in the Magimix bowl and process until the herbs are finely chopped. Add the fat bacon and liver and process until the meat is very finely chopped. Remove the bacon, liver and herbs to a mixing bowl. Place the veal in the Magimix bowl with the onion and garlic, add a pinch of mace and season with salt and freshly ground black pepper. Process until the veal is finely chopped.

Add the egg, cream and melted butter and continue to process until the ingredients are well mixed.

Add the veal to the ingredients in a mixing bowl and pour over the red wine. Mix the ingredients well.

Line a terrine with the thin rashers of bacon. Press the ingredients firmly into the terrine and fold over any ends of bacon. Top with three bay leaves and cover tightly with foil. Place in a baking tin with enough hot water to come half way up the sides of the terrine and bake in a moderate oven (180°C, 350°F, Reg. 4) for $1\frac{1}{2}$–2 hours until the sides of the pâté have come away from the terrine.

Weight down, cool and then chill in a refrigerator for at least 8 hours before cutting into slices and serving with hot toast or French bread.

Scrambled eggs with smoked salmon

Serves 4

This makes an excellent first course but it can also be served as a luncheon or supper dish. Take care not to overprocess the eggs.

Smoked salmon trimmings are ideal for this dish and much more reasonable in price than the slices.

175 g (6 oz) smoked
 salmon
8 eggs
1.5 dl ($\frac{1}{4}$ pint) single cream

salt and freshly ground
 black pepper
50 g (2 oz) butter

Cut one-third of the smoked salmon into thin matchstick strips for garnishing.

USE THE
METAL BLADE

Place the remaining smoked salmon in the Magimix bowl and process until the smoked salmon is roughly chopped. Add the eggs and 2 tablespoons cream, season with just a little salt and a generous amount of freshly ground black pepper and process for just long enough to break up the eggs.

Melt the butter in a small, heavy pan. Add the egg mixture and cook over a low heat, stirring gently every now and then until the eggs are just set.

Divide the eggs between four warm plates. Heat the remaining cream to boiling point, pour it over the eggs and garnish with the strips of smoked salmon.
Serve at once.

Welsh rarebit

Serves 4

150 g (5 oz) Cheddar
 cheese
25 g (1 oz) butter
1 tablespoon flour
3 tablespoons milk

2 tablespoons light ale
1 teaspoon Dijon mustard
salt and freshly ground
 black pepper

USE THE
METAL BLADE

Break the cheese into pieces. Combine the cheese and the other ingredients in the Magimix bowl, season with salt and freshly ground black pepper and process until reduced to a paste.

Spread the rarebit on buttered slices of toast and cook under a hot grill until bubbling and golden brown.

Crumpet rarebits

Serves 6

100 g (4 oz) Cheddar cheese
1 tablespoon mango
   chutney
½ teaspoon Worcestershire
   sauce

½ teaspoon made English
   mustard
37 g (1½ oz) softened butter
6 crumpets

USE THE
METAL BLADE

Roughly break up the cheese and put it in the Magimix bowl with the remaining ingredients. Process until the mixture has become a smooth paste.

Spread the cheese paste on top of six crumpets, place on a baking sheet and bake in a hot oven (220°C, 425°F, Reg. 7) for 5–6 minutes until the cheese has melted and is bubbling and the crumpets are crisp.

Cabbage leaves with a mushroom and spinach filling

Serves 4

8 large leaves from a
   Savoy cabbage
50 g (2 oz) Cheddar cheese
225 g (½ lb) frozen spinach
100 g (4 oz) white bread
   with the crusts removed

100 g (4 oz) mushrooms
3 egg yolks
salt, pepper and a pinch
   ground nutmeg
37 g (1½ oz) butter
1.5 dl (¼ pint) chicken stock

Wash and dry the leaves and blanch them in boiling, salted water for 5 minutes. Drain the leaves well and pat them dry on kitchen paper. Remove the thick end of the stalks from the leaves.

Roughly chop the cheese.

Cook the spinach in very little boiling, salted water until tender and drain really well.

USE THE
METAL BLADE

Place the bread and cheese in the Magimix bowl and process until the bread is reduced to coarse breadcrumbs. Add the mushrooms, egg yolks and spinach to the bowl with the bread and cheese, season with salt, freshly ground black pepper and a pinch of nutmeg and process until the eggs are beaten and the mushrooms are finely chopped.

Divide the filling between the eight cabbage leaves and roll the leaves up into neat parcels.

50

Place the rolls in a well buttered baking dish, pour over the stock, dot with the remaining butter, cover with foil and bake in a moderate oven (180°C, 350°F, Reg. 4) for 30 minutes.

Vegetables for crudités

Crudités can be served as a first course or with cocktails or drinks. Arrange a colourful platter of prepared raw vegetables and serve them with one or a combination of the dip recipes.

Small hard-boiled eggs and thin slices of salami can be added to the ingredients.

RAW VEGETABLES
1. Carrots, peeled and cut into thin matchstick strips.
2. Green and red peppers, cut into thin strips.
3. Small, whole, tomatoes.
4. Thick sticks of peeled cucumber.
5. Florettes of cauliflower.
6. Sticks of small, unpeeled, courgettes.
7. Sticks of tender celery stalks.
8. Trimmed spring onions.
9. Quartered chicory.

Serve the crudités with hot French bread and butter.

Small mousses of chicken livers

Serves 4

Rich but at the same time light and with a sophisticated flavour. Serve the mousses with a little tomato sauce over the top of each one. (Tomato sauce see page 158.)

12 g (½ oz) butter
1 tablespoon flour
1.5 dl (¼ pint) milk
225 g (8 oz) chicken livers
1 egg
1 egg yolk
3 tablespoons double cream
1 tablespoon brandy
salt and freshly ground black pepper

Melt the butter in a small saucepan. Add the flour and mix well. Gradually blend in the milk, stirring continually over a medium high heat until the sauce comes to the boil and is thick and smooth.

Remove any fibres or yellow patches from the chicken livers.

51

Combine the livers, sauce, egg, egg yolk, cream and brandy in the Magimix bowl, season with salt and freshly ground black pepper and process until the ingredients are smooth.

Divide the mousse between four buttered cocotte dishes, stand them in a baking tin filled with enough hot water to come half way up the sides of the dishes and bake in a moderate oven (180°C, 350°F, Reg. 4) for 30 minutes until the mousses are firmly set.

Spoon over a little tomato sauce and serve at once.

Mushrooms with sour cream

Serves 4

This is such a good dish that it can well be served as a first course garnished with triangles of crisply fried bread.

2 sprigs parsley	*salt and a pinch of paprika*
1 small onion	*½ tablespoon flour*
450 g (1 lb) firm button	*1 carton (1.5 dl/5 fl. oz)*
mushrooms	*sour cream*
37 g (1½ oz) butter	

USE THE
METAL BLADE

Place the parsley in the Magimix bowl and process until finely chopped. Remove the parsley.

Peel and quarter the onion, place it in the Magimix bowl and process until finely chopped. Remove the onion.

USE THE
SLICING DISC

Slice the mushrooms with the slicing disc.

Heat the butter in a frying pan, add the onion and cook over a low heat until the onion is soft and transparent. Add the sliced mushrooms and continue to cook for about 4 minutes until the mushrooms are tender but not too soft. Add the parsley and season with salt and paprika. Mix the flour with the sour cream, pour it over the mushrooms, bring to the boil and simmer for 3 minutes, stirring gently.

Shrimp toast

Serves 4

I first came across this recipe when I was working on the menus of a restaurant called Mr Chow's in London. I used to make it at home and it took hours of chopping and pounding to get the ingredients to the right consistency.

Now, with the help of my Magimix food processor it takes only minutes to make an unusual first course which is popular with everyone.

small piece of fresh ginger (available in good greengrocers)
6 water chestnuts (these can be bought in tins)
225 g ($\frac{1}{2}$ lb) peeled prawns
1 spring onion
1 egg yolk

1$\frac{1}{2}$ teaspoons cornflour (cornstarch)
1 tablespoon medium dry sherry
salt and freshly ground black pepper
2 egg whites
3 slices white bread
oil for frying

USE THE METAL BLADE

Peel and chop the ginger.

Place the water chestnuts and the ginger in the Magimix bowl and process until the ingredients are finely ground. Add the prawns, the spring onion, roughly chopped, and the egg yolk and process until the ingredients are ground to a paste. Add the cornflour and sherry and continue to process until the ingredients are smooth. Season with salt and freshly ground black pepper and turn the Magimix on and off to mix in the seasonings. Turn the mixture into a bowl.

Whip the egg whites until stiff and lightly fold whites into the prawn mixture. Spread the prawn mixture on the bread slices. Remove the crusts and cut each slice into four thin fingers.

Heat 1 cm ($\frac{1}{2}$ in.) vegetable oil in a frying pan. Add the bread fingers, prawn side down and fry over a high heat until golden brown. Turn over and continue to fry until the other side of the fingers is crisp. Drain on kitchen paper and serve at once.

Ham mousse

Serves 4 as a first course, 2 as a main

A smooth, light mousse which makes the best possible use of 225 g (8 oz) of ham.

1 tablespoon flour
1.5 dl ($\frac{1}{4}$ pint) milk
225 g (8 oz) cooked ham
1 teaspoon made English mustard

19 g ($\frac{3}{4}$ oz) butter
1 egg
1 egg yolk
a pinch of cayenne

Melt the butter in a saucepan. Add the flour and mix well. Gradually blend in the milk, stirring continually over a medium heat until the sauce comes to the boil and is thick and smooth. Remove from the heat and leave to cool.

USE THE
METAL BLADE

Roughly chop the ham, put it in the Magimix bowl and process until the ham is reduced to a smooth paste. Scrape down the sides of the bowl with the plastic spatula if necessary.

Add the sauce, mustard and eggs to the ham and season with cayenne pepper. Process until the ingredients are smooth.

Generously butter four ramekin dishes. Spoon in the ham mixture and top with buttered foil. Put into a bain marie, half fill with hot water and bake in a moderate oven (180°C, 350°F, Reg. 4) for 30–35 minutes until set firm.

Remove the ramekins from the bain marie, leave to cool for 5 minutes and then turn upside down and tap to turn out. Serve hot or cold with tomato sauce.

Mock caviare

Serves 4

This is a dish which goes under many names and has been claimed as their invention by many Mediterranean and Balkan countries where aubergines grow almost wild. It makes an inexpensive first course or can be served as a dip with drinks. The garlic is essential to my way of thinking but if you don't like garlic just cut it out.

1 large aubergine
1 medium onion
2 cloves garlic
1 small green pepper
juice of ½ lemon

1.5 dl (¼ pint) olive oil
salt and freshly ground
black pepper
few drops Tabasco sauce
chopped parsley

USE THE
METAL BLADE

Put the aubergine in a grill pan and under a high heat. Cook the aubergine, turning frequently, until it is blackened on the outside and soft to the touch. Leave until cool enough to handle.

Peel and quarter the onion. Peel the garlic cloves.

Remove the core and seeds of the green pepper and roughly chop the flesh. Slide off the peel of the aubergine and roughly chop the flesh.

Combine aubergine, onion, garlic, pepper, lemon juice and olive oil in the Magimix bowl and process until the mixture has become a coarse purée. Season with salt and

54

pepper, add a few drops of Tabasco sauce and switch the Magimix food processor on and off to mix in the seasonings.

Pile the purée in a pyramid onto a serving dish, sprinkle over a little chopped parsley and serve with hot toast or French bread.

Avacamo

Serves 6

A smooth blend of avocados and tuna which is delicious with hot toast or hot salt biscuits. For a buffet party try serving bowls of avacamo with taramasalata and mock caviar. In glass bowls these look attractive and make an interesting and delicious combination.

2 medium, ripe avocados
1 small tin tuna fish
1 spring onion
1 teaspoon lemon juice

1.5 dl ($\frac{1}{4}$ pint) mayonnaise
few drops Tabasco sauce
salt and freshly ground
    black pepper

USE THE
METAL BLADE

Peel the avocados and cut into four pieces. Drain the tuna and roughly chop the spring onion. Place the avocados in the Magimix bowl with the tuna, lemon juice, mayonnaise, Tabasco and spring onion. Season with salt and pepper and process until the mixture is smooth and light.

Taramasalata with prawns in green pepper cups

Serves 4

100 g (4 oz) white bread
    with the crusts removed
1 clove garlic
75 g (3 oz) smoked cod's
    roe
juice of $\frac{1}{2}$ lemon
1.5 dl ($\frac{1}{4}$ pint) olive oil

2 tablespoons yoghurt
1 tablespoon chopped
    chives
freshly ground black pepper
50 g (2 oz) peeled prawns
2 green peppers
twists of lemon for garnish

Soak bread in warm water until soft and squeeze out excess water.

Peel and roughly chop the garlic.

USE THE
METAL BLADE

Combine the bread, garlic and cod's roe in the Magimix bowl and process until the ingredients form a smooth paste. Add the lemon juice and switch on and off to mix.

55

With the machine switched on, gradually add the olive oil, a little at a time in the same way as when making mayonnaise, until all the oil is absorbed into the cod's roe paste. Add the yoghurt and chives, season with ground pepper and process for just long enough to mix the ingredients. Add the prawns and process again until the prawns are coarsely chopped.

Halve the peppers and if necessary cut a sliver off each end so that they stand firmly. Using a small sharp knife cut out the core and seeds. Fill the pepper halves with the taramasalata and chill before serving.

Garnish each serving with a twist of lemon and serve with hot toast or hot French bread.

Jellied tomato ring with prawns and watercress

Serves 6

675 g (1½ lb) ripe tomatoes
salt, pepper and pinch sugar
pinch dried basil and oregano
1 small bunch chives

1 tablespoon gelatine powder
juice of ½ a lemon
pinch cayenne pepper
170 g (6 oz) prawns
1.5 dl (¼ pint) mayonnaise
1 bunch watercress
vinaigrette dressing

Cover the tomatoes with boiling water and leave them to stand for 2 minutes. Drain off the water and slide off the tomato skins. Halve the tomatoes and remove the hard core and seeds with a small spoon.

Combine the tomatoes in a saucepan with the sugar and a seasoning of salt and freshly ground black pepper. Add the herbs, bring to the boil, cover and simmer, stirring occasionally, for 30 minutes until the tomatoes are reduced to a soft, dry pulp. Measure the pulp to 6 dl (1 pint) and leave to cool. Any extra pulp can be added to soups, stews or sauces.

USE THE METAL BLADE

Place the chives in the Magimix bowl and process until the chives are finely chopped.

Cover the gelatine with 15 ml (1 tablespoon) boiling water and stir until the gelatine has dissolved. Add the lemon juice and mix well. Add the tomatoes and gelatine mixture to the chives, season with cayenne pepper and process until the ingredients are smooth. Pour the tomato mixture into a ring mould and chill in a refrigerator until set firm. Turn out the tomato ring.

Fill the ring with the prawns mixed with the mayonnaise and top with a little more cayenne pepper.

Surround the ring with the watercress dipped in the vinaigrette dressing and serve well chilled.

Salmon and celeriac rémoulade

Serves 6

A delicious starter. Try and buy cheap trimmings for the smoked salmon.

450 g (1 lb) celeriac
1 teaspoon salt
2 teaspoons lemon juice
3 teaspoons Dijon
  mustard
3 tablespoons boiling
  water
1.5 dl ($\frac{1}{4}$ pint) olive oil

1 tablespoon white wine
  vinegar
salt and freshly ground
  black pepper
100 g (4 oz) smoked
  salmon
cayenne pepper

USE THE
GRATING DISC

Peel the celeriac root and cut into pieces small enough to fit into the feed tube. Shred the celeriac with the shredding disc. Remove the celeriac to a bowl and sprinkle over 1 teaspoon of salt and the lemon juice to prevent the celeriac turning brown. Leave for 30 minutes then rinse in cold water and pat dry on kitchen paper.

USE THE
PLASTIC BLADE

Put the mustard in the Magimix bowl, switch on and pour in the boiling water through the feed tube while the machine is running. Gradually add the olive oil in a slow thin stream and continue to process until the sauce is thick and well emulsified. Gradually pour in the vinegar and add a seasoning of salt and pepper.

Turn the sauce into a bowl and add the celeriac.

Cut twelve matchstick strips of smoked salmon about 5 cm (2 in.) long. Put the remaining smoked salmon in the Magimix bowl and process for a very short time to just chop the salmon.

Add the salmon to the celeriac and sauce and mix lightly to combine the ingredients.

Pile the mixture onto six individual bowls (you can place it on crisp lettuce leaves), top each serving with two crossed strips of smoked salmon, sprinkle with just a little cayenne pepper and chill in a refrigerator for at least 2 hours before serving.

Sardine stuffed lemons

Serves 6

This makes a good summer starter when lemons are cheap. The thick skinned lemons which are not so good for squeezing are best for this dish.

6 large lemons
100 g (4 oz) butter
1 tin sardines in tomato
*   sauce*

1 teaspoon Dijon mustard
salt and 2 teaspoons
*   paprika pepper*

Cut a thin slice off the bottom of the lemons. Cut a thicker slice off the top of the lemons and scoop out the flesh with a sharp edged spoon. Remove any tough membranes and the pips and reserve the juice and pulp.

USE THE
METAL BLADE

Place the butter in the Magimix bowl and process until soft and creamy. Add the sardines, tomato sauce, lemon pulp and juice and mustard. Season with salt and paprika and process until the ingredients are smooth. Spoon the sardine mixture into the lemons, replace the slices from the tops and chill well before serving.

Accompany the lemons with Melba toast or thin slices of buttered brown bread.

Fish dishes

Couronne rose de poisson

Serves 8

A most sophisticated mould of fish flavoured with tomatoes and served with a mayonnaise verte.

1 onion
1 carrot
fish bones and skin
bouquet garni
salt and freshly ground
  black pepper
1 glass white wine
450 g (1 lb) cod or firm
  flesh white fish
450 g (1 lb) firm ripe
  tomatoes
37 g (1½ oz) butter
1 small bunch parsley and
  chervil

1 sprig tarragon
2 cloves garlic
1 small bunch chives
1 tablespoon tomato purée
pinch ground cloves,
  ginger and nutmeg
4 large eggs
5 tablespoons double cream
few drops Tabasco sauce
3 dl (½ pint) mayonnaise
  verte (see page 152)
100 g (4 oz) peeled prawns

Peel and roughly chop the onion and carrot. Place the fish bones and skin in a saucepan with the onion, bouquet garni and carrot; season with salt and pepper, pour over the white wine and enough water to cover the ingredients, bring to the boil and simmer for 30 minutes. Drain the liquid through a fine sieve.

Cover the fish with the stock, bring to the boil and simmer for 15 minutes or until the fish is just tender.

Cover the tomatoes with boiling water. Leave to stand for 2 minutes, drain and then slide off the tomato skins. Halve the tomatoes, scoop out the core and seeds with a small spoon and roughly chop the flesh. Melt the butter in a saucepan. Add the tomatoes and cook over a low heat, stirring every now and then, for 15 minutes.

Remove the tough stalks from the herbs; peel the garlic cloves.

USE THE
METAL BLADE Place the herbs in the Magimix bowl and process until the herbs are finely chopped.

Combine the fish, tomatoes, garlic, tomato purée, spices, eggs, cream and Tabasco with the herbs in the Magimix bowl, season with salt and pepper and process until the ingredients are smooth.

Line a ring mould with well oiled foil. Pour the fish mixture into the mould and set it in a baking dish. Pour in enough boiling water to come half way up the sides of the mould and bake in a moderately hot oven (190°C, 375°F, Reg. 5) for 30 minutes. Leave the mousse to cool in its mould and then chill in a refrigerator.

Turn out the mould and gently remove the foil. Fill the centre with the mayonnaise verte and decorate with peeled prawns.

Fish mayonnaise with red peppers and celery

Serves 4

This makes a very good summer salad. It is unusual and versatile. Serve the salad as a first course, or as a main course, or use it as a centrepiece of a hot weather buffet party. Accompany the salad with sliced cucumber in a dressing and a green salad.

3 stalks celery
3 dl ($\frac{1}{2}$ pint) mayonnaise
  (see page 147)
salt, freshly ground pepper
pinch cayenne
lettuce leaves

450 g (1 lb) cooked white
  fish (turbot is best of all
  but you can use plaice,
  halibut, cod or filleted
  whiting etc.)
1 red pepper

Remove the skin and bones from the fish. Halve the pepper, remove the core and seeds and roughly chop the flesh. Roughly chop the celery stalks and leaves.

Place the red pepper and celery in the Magimix bowl and process until the ingredients are roughly chopped. Add the mayonnaise and fish to the chopped ingredients and season with salt, freshly ground black pepper and a pinch of cayenne. Switch on and off two or three times to mix the ingredients – do not over process.

Arrange some lettuce leaves on a serving dish and pile the fish salad in the centre of the leaves. Chill before serving.

Potato and tuna fish patties

Serves 6–8

Delicious potato cakes flavoured with parsley, tuna and onion. Serve them topped with a fried egg or with tomato sauce.

1 bunch parsley
1 small onion
1 small tin tuna fish
675 g (1½ lb) cooked
*   potatoes*

salt and freshly ground
*   black pepper*
lard, dripping or bacon fat
*   for frying*

Remove the tough stalks from the parsley. Peel and quarter the onion. Drain the tuna fish.

Place the parsley in the Magimix bowl and process until the leaves are finely chopped. Add the onion, potatoes and tuna fish and continue to process until the ingredients are well mixed. Season with salt and pepper and switch the machine on and off to mix the seasoning into the ingredients.

Remove the mixture from the bowl and, using floured hands, shape into ten flat patties about 6 mm (¼ in.) thick and 7.5 cm (3 in.) in diameter.

Heat some lard, dripping or bacon fat in a saucepan until smoking. Add the patties and cook over a high heat for about 5 minutes on each side until the patties are well browned and cooked through. Drain on kitchen paper before serving.

Quenelles

Serves 4

This most sophisticated dish once needed hours of pounding by hand in order to reach the fine texture which makes it one of the great classics of haute cuisine. Now all the hard work is done by your Magimix and the result should be poached dumplings of the most delicate lightness.

225 g (8 oz) boned and skinned white fish with the bones removed (use turbot, halibut, hake, cod or pike etc.)
50 g (2 oz) Gruyère cheese
salt, pepper and a pinch ground nutmeg

3 dl ($\frac{1}{2}$ pint) double cream
50 g (2 oz) butter
100 g (4 oz) peeled prawns
1$\frac{1}{2}$ tablespoons flour
4.5 dl ($\frac{3}{4}$ pint) milk

USE THE
METAL BLADE

Roughly chop the cheese and process it in the Magimix bowl until it is finely powdered. Remove the cheese. Cut the fish into 2.5 cm (1 in.) cubes and place them in the Magimix bowl. Process until the fish is reduced to a smooth paste. Season with salt, pepper and a pinch of nutmeg, add the cream and process for a further 20 seconds. Remove from the bowl and chill in the refrigerator for thirty minutes until the mixture is stiff.

Roll the fish mixture on a well floured board to a thin sausage shape and cut into pieces two inches long. Poach the quenelles in 2 l (4 pints) boiling salted water or fish stock. As soon as they rise to the surface of the water, remove the quenelles with a slotted spoon and arrange them in a lightly buttered baking dish. Sprinkle prawns over the top.

Melt the butter in a saucepan. Add the flour and mix well, gradually blend in the milk, stirring continually over a medium high heat until the sauce comes to the boil and is thick and smooth. Add three quarters of the cheese, season with salt and pepper and simmer for three minutes, stirring every now and then.

Pour the sauce over the quenelles and prawns, sprinkle over the remaining cheese and bake in a hot oven (200°C, 400°F, Reg. 6) for about 15 minutes until the dish is hot through and the top is golden brown.

Fish pâté

A mixture of white and smoked fish.

4 sprigs parsley
2 small onions
350 g (12 oz) white fish
   fillets (cod, haddock etc.)
75 g (3 oz) butter
1 clove garlic, white pepper
2 anchovy fillets

juice of 1 small lemon
350 g (12 oz) smoked
   haddock or cod
1 bay leaf
bouquet garni
4 black peppercorns
salt and cayenne pepper

Remove the stalks from the parsley. Peel and quarter one onion. Peel and roughly chop the second onion. Remove the skin from the white fish and roughly chop the flesh.

USE THE
METAL BLADE

Place the parsley leaves in the Magimix bowl and process until the leaves are finely chopped. Remove the parsley.

Place the quartered onion in the Magimix bowl and process until the onion is finely chopped. Remove the onion, place the white fish in the Magimix bowl and process until the fish is chopped.

Melt 37 g ($1\frac{1}{2}$ oz) butter in a frying pan. Add the onion and cook over a low heat until the onion is soft and transparent. Add the white fish and cook over a high heat, stirring, for 3 minutes until the fish is just cooked. Transfer the onions and fish to the Magimix bowl, season with white pepper, add the anchovy fillets, half the parsley and half the lemon juice and process until the ingredients are reduced to a smooth paste. Remove the ingredients and leave to cool.

Place the smoked haddock or cod in a saucepan with the bay leaf, bouquet garni, peppercorns and chopped onion. Cover with water, bring to the boil and simmer for about 8 minutes until the fish is just tender. Drain, remove the fish and discard any skin and bones.

Combine the hot fish with the remaining butter, parsley and lemon juice in the Magimix bowl, season with salt and a little cayenne pepper and process until the ingredients are smooth. Leave to cool.

Spread a third of the cooled white fish pâté in a terrine, cover with a third of the smoked fish pâté and continue the layers. Press the ingredients firmly into the terrine, cover with foil and chill until firmly set. Turn out and serve with hot toast.

Herrings with apples and potatoes

Serves 4

An aromatic way of using these inexpensive fish.

3 medium potatoes, peeled
2 cooking apples
37 g (1½ oz) butter or
  margarine

4 herrings, filleted
salt and freshly ground
  black pepper

Peel the potatoes, peel, core and roughly chop the apples.

USE THE
SLICING DISC

Slice the potatoes through the slicing disc.

USE THE
METAL BLADE

Place the apples in the Magimix bowl and process until the apples are roughly chopped (to about the size of small peas).

Grease a baking dish. Arrange slices of potato over the bottom and around the sides of the dish. Put half the fillets in the bottom of the dish, sprinkle over some of the chopped apples and season with salt and freshly ground black pepper. Fill the dish with alternate layers of fish and apples and top with the remaining potatoes. Sprinkle with a little more salt and pepper and dot with the butter or margarine left over from greasing the dish.

Cover with foil and bake in a moderate oven (180°C, 350°F, Reg. 4) for 45 minutes. Remove the foil and return to the oven for a further 5 minutes to brown the top.

Mackerel with souffléd mayonnaise sauce

Serves 6

25 g (1 oz) butter
1 tablespoon Dijon
  mustard
6 mackerel, filleted
1 small bunch parsley

4 tablespoons mixed
  pickles
1.5 dl (¼ pint) mayonnaise
1 tablespoon lemon juice
salt and cayenne pepper
2 egg whites

USE THE
METAL BLADE

Combine the butter and mustard and process until the mixture is smooth. Remove the butter and clean bowl.

Spread the butter thinly on the inside of the mackerel fillets and grill them under a medium high heat for 6–8 minutes until the fillets are cooked. Place the fillets in a fireproof serving dish.

Remove the tough stalks from the parsley and place the leaves in the Magimix bowl. Process until the parsley is finely chopped. Add the pickles, mayonnaise and lemon juice, season with salt and cayenne pepper and continue to process until the pickles are finely chopped.

Beat the egg whites until stiff and fold in the mayonnaise mixture. Spread the sauce over the fish and return to a medium high grill. Cook for about 5 minutes or until the sauce is puffed up and golden.

Shellfish flan

Serves 6

Mussels and shrimps in a rich saffron cream filling.

¼ teaspoon strand saffron
1 tablespoon hot water
20 cm (8 in.) flan case
  lined with pâté brisée
  (see page 179)
1 tin mussels in brine or
  12 cooked mussels

175 g (6 oz) peeled
  prawns
3 dl (½ pint) double cream
3 eggs
salt and freshly ground
  black pepper
pinch nutmeg

Cover the saffron with the hot water and leave to stand for 15 minutes. Drain off the liquid, pressing the saffron with a teaspoon.

Line the pastry case with foil or greaseproof paper and fill with dried or metal beans. Bake the case 'blind' in a preheated hot oven (200°C, 400°F, Reg. 6) for 10 minutes. Remove the case and take out the beans and paper or foil.

Arrange the drained mussels and prawns in the flan case.

USE THE
METAL BLADE

Combine the cream, eggs and saffron water in the Magimix bowl. Season with salt, pepper and a small pinch ground nutmeg and process until the ingredients are smooth.

Pour the filling over the shellfish and bake in a moderately hot oven (190°C, 375°F, Reg. 5) for 30 minutes until set.

Serve hot or cold.

Mould of white fish and prawns

Serves 4–6

450 g (1 lb) filleted plaice
   with the bones
1 small onion
1 bay leaf
salt and freshly ground
   black pepper
1.5 dl ($\frac{1}{4}$ pint) white wine
1 small bunch parsley
12 g ($\frac{1}{2}$ oz) gelatine powder

3 tablespoons warm water
1 egg
3 tablespoons double cream
1 teaspoon lemon juice
2 tablespoons mayonnaise
pinch nutmeg and cayenne
   pepper
100 g (4 oz) peeled
   prawns

Combine the fish bones with the onion, peeled and roughly chopped and the bay leaf, season with salt and pepper, pour over the wine and enough water to cover, bring to the boil and simmer for 20 minutes. Drain off the fish stock.

Steam the fish fillets over boiling water for about 10 minutes until just tender and remove any tough skin.

Remove the tough stalks from the parsley.

Dissolve the gelatine in 3 tablespoons warm water.

USE THE
METAL BLADE

Place the parsley leaves in the Magimix bowl and process until the leaves are finely chopped. Remove the leaves.

Place the egg in the Magimix bowl and process until smooth. Add 3 dl ($\frac{1}{2}$ pint) of fish stock and the cream and process until well mixed. Turn into a small heavy pan and cook over a low heat, stirring continually, until the sauce thickens enough to coat the back of a spoon. Leave to cool.

Return the sauce to the Magimix bowl and add the fish, gelatine mixture and lemon juice. Add the mayonnaise, season with salt, nutmeg and a little cayenne and process until the mixture is fairly smooth. Turn into a damp mould and chill in a refrigerator until set. Turn out and garnish with a little sprinkling of cayenne pepper and the prawns.

West Coast fish mousse

Serves 6–8

A delicious cold dish to serve for a buffet party, as an extra special first course or as a main course for a hot summer day's luncheon. Make the mould in a ring shape and you can ring the changes almost indefinitely with the filling you put in the centre – see end of recipe for suggestions.

1 packet 12 g ($\frac{1}{2}$ oz)
  gelatine powder
3 tablespoons boiling water
2 hard-boiled eggs
1 small avocado
450 g (1 lb) cold cooked
  white fleshed fish (plaice,
  bass, flounder, grey
  mullet etc.)
1 small green pepper

4.8 dl (16 fl oz)
  mayonnaise (see page
  147) or use a good
  commercial brand
1 tablespoon tomato
  ketchup
few drops Worcestershire
  sauce
few drops Tabasco sauce
salt and freshly ground
  black pepper

Pour the hot water over the gelatine, mix well and leave to dissolve and cool.

Peel and roughly chop the hard-boiled eggs. Peel and roughly chop the avocado. Remove any skin and bones from the fish. Remove the core and seeds from the green pepper and roughly chop the flesh.

USE THE
METAL BLADE

Combine the mayonnaise, tomato ketchup, Worcestershire sauce, Tabasco sauce and avocado in the Magimix bowl and process until the ingredients are well mixed and the avocado is puréed into the mayonnaise.

Add the eggs, green pepper and fish, season with salt and freshly ground black pepper, pour in the dissolved gelatine and process for just long enough to mix the ingredients and finely chop the green pepper – the mixture should still have plenty of texture to it and not be too smooth.

Turn the mixture into a damp ring mould and chill for 1 hour. Dip into hot water, turn out and fill the centre of the ring with any of the following:

1. Chopped avocado mixed with a vinaigrette dressing.
2. Peeled prawns tossed in a vinaigrette dressing.
3. Watercress leaves tossed in a vinaigrette dressing.
4. A salad of new potatoes with small pieces of crisply fried bacon and finely chopped chives tossed in a curried vinaigrette dressing.

Coulibiac

Serves 6–8

Authentically this is a dish which should be made with uncooked salmon. In my more frugal interpretation of an original recipe, cod is substituted for the salmon and prawns are added for colour and flavour. I serve it with a tomato sauce, to which some peeled prawns have been added.

100 g (4 oz) long grain rice
1 small onion
1 bunch parsley
25 g (1 oz) butter
2 small eggs
2 anchovy fillets
juice of ½ a lemon, grated
*   rind of 1 lemon*

450 g (1 lb) cooked cod
*   with the bones and skin*
*   removed*
salt, freshly ground black
*   pepper and a pinch of*
*   cayenne*
450 g (1 lb) flaky pastry
*   (see page 178)*
50 g (2 oz) peeled prawns
little beaten egg

USE THE
METAL BLADE

Cook the rice in boiling salted water until tender, drain, rinse in cold water and drain well. Peel and roughly chop the onion. Remove the coarse stalks from the parsley.

Place the onion in the Magimix bowl and process until the onion is finely chopped. Remove the onion with the plastic spatula making sure all the pieces are removed from the bowl.

Melt the butter, add the onion and cook over a low heat until the onion is soft and transparent. Leave to cool.

Place the parsley leaves in the Magimix bowl and process until the leaves are finely chopped. Add the eggs and anchovy fillets to the parsley and process until the eggs are beaten. Add the lemon juice and rind, fish, rice and onion, season with salt and freshly ground black pepper and a pinch of cayenne. Process for just long enough to mix the ingredients.

Roll out just over a third of the pastry into a rectangle about 15 × 30 cm (6 × 12 in.). Put the pastry base on a sheet of greased foil. Place the fish mixture on the pastry base and shape it into a neat loaf shape leaving 1 cm (½ in.) on all sides.

Place the prawns on top of the fish mixture. Roll out the remaining pastry to an oblong about 7.5 cm (3 in.) larger than the base. Cover the fish, damp the edges of the pastry, press down firmly and trim off any rough edges. Brush the pastry with beaten egg and bake in a hot oven (220°C, 425°F, Reg. 7) for 10 minutes then lower the heat to moderate (180°C, 350°F, Reg. 4) and continue to cook for a further 40 minutes. Cover the pie with a sheet of damp greaseproof paper if it begins to brown too much.

Serve hot.

Marinade for fish

Use this for any fish that is to be grilled or wrapped in foil and baked. It is particularly good for those giant prawns, for salmon steaks, whole mullet, mackerel and bass.

1 onion
6 cloves garlic
1 in. piece of fresh ginger root
6 tablespoons olive or vegetable oil
juice of 1½ lemons

2 green chillis
¼ teaspoon cayenne pepper
1 teaspoon turmeric
¼ teaspoon fennel seeds
salt and freshly ground black pepper

Peel and quarter the onion. Peel the garlic. Peel and chop the ginger root.

USE THE
METAL BLADE

Combine all the ingredients in the Magimix bowl, season with salt and pepper and process until the onion is reduced to a pulp.

Peel and de-vein giant prawns. Clean whole fish but leave the head on and lightly score through the skin in diagonal cuts about 1 cm (½ in.) apart. Place prawns, steaks or whole fish in a dish, pour over the marinade and leave for at least 4 hours before cooking.

Egg dishes

Using your Magimix food processor when preparing egg dishes

Some of the simplest and best classic dishes in the world are made from an egg base. In almost all of these dishes your Magimix food processor can help to make dishes of perfection and take the hard work out of many fiddly preparations which go into the dishes.

Your Magimix food processor knocks up an omelette or scrambled egg mixture which is as good as any made by a French chef. With the Magimix food processor you can master the art of successful soufflés, roulades or timbales, and both hot and cold dishes made with a base of stuffed eggs become child's play.

POINTS TO WATCH

Do not over-process eggs which are to be used in omelettes or scrambled eggs – they should never become fluffy while in the Magimix bowl.

Add seasonings at the end of the processing.

70

Eggs à l'Indienne

Serves 4–6

A light lunch dish or starter of hard-boiled eggs stuffed with a light curry mixture and masked in a delicately lemon flavoured mayonnaise.

6 hard-boiled eggs
1 teaspoon curry powder
1 tablespoon tarragon
* vinegar*
4 leaves fresh tarragon

2.4 dl (8 fl. oz) home-made
* mayonnaise (see page*
* 147)*
salt and freshly ground
* black pepper*
1 teaspoon lemon juice
cayenne pepper

USE THE
METAL BLADE

Slice the eggs in half lengthwise and gently remove the yolks.

Place the egg yolks in the Magimix bowl and add the curry powder, tarragon vinegar, tarragon leaves and 2 table-spoons mayonnaise. Season with salt and freshly ground black pepper and process until the mixture is smooth.
    Combine the remaining mayonnaise with the lemon juice and mix well.
    Fill the egg whites with the curry mixture and place the eggs, cut side down on a bed of lettuce leaves. Mask the eggs with the mayonnaise and sprinkle over a little cayenne pepper.

Stuffed eggs

These are very versatile delicacies. Serve them as a glorified egg mayonnaise, masked with a delicious mayonnaise made in your Magimix food processor, take them on picnics, use them as part of a summer buffet table or serve small eggs with drinks at a cocktail party.

71

Stuffed eggs with anchovies and prawns

Serves 4

4 hard-boiled eggs
50 g (2 oz) peeled prawns
5 anchovy fillets
37 g (1½ oz) softened butter

white pepper
2 tablespoons double cream
chopped chives

Peel and halve the hard-boiled eggs and scoop out the yolks. Cut a thin sliver from the bottom of the egg white halves to make them stand steadily.

USE THE
METAL BLADE

Place the prawns in the Magimix bowl and process until finely chopped. Remove the prawns.

Combine the egg yolks, anchovies and butter in the Magimix bowl and season with a little white pepper. Process until the mixture is reduced to a smooth purée. Add the cream and switch on and off to incorporate the ingredients.

Using a small teaspoon, press the prawns into the bottom of the egg white halves and top with the anchovy mixture, shaping it into a dome over the top of the egg white halves.

Garnish with finely chopped chives.

Alternative fillings for hard-boiled eggs

1. Process the egg yolks with 6 stuffed olives and 3 tablespoons mayonnaise before stuffing the white halves.

2. Process the egg yolks with 2 sardines, one chopped spring onion, 1 tablespoon tomato ketchup and 1 tablespoon cream before stuffing the white halves.

3. Process the egg yolks with 1 small smoked trout (with the skin and bones removed), a few drops of lemon juice and 2 tablespoons sour cream seasoned with salt and pepper before stuffing the white halves.

Baked eggs

Baked eggs are amongst my favourite recipes to serve as a quick supper dish or a first course when timing is of no importance – they have to be served as soon as they are cooked!

With your Magimix food processor you can incorporate the most exciting flavours into the basic baked egg recipe.

Basic baked egg recipe

Serves 4

50 g (2 oz) butter
8 eggs

salt and freshly ground
black pepper
4 tablespoons double cream

Melt the butter in a saucepan and pour it into four ramekin dishes that are large enough to take two eggs each with about 1 cm ($\frac{1}{2}$ in.) leeway at the top. Break the eggs into the dishes and season with salt and freshly ground black pepper. Place the ramekins in a moderate oven (180°C, 350°F, Reg. 4) and cook for about 8 minutes until the eggs are just set. Pour over the cream and serve at once.

Variations for baked eggs

Baked eggs with bacon

2 rashers streaky bacon

basic baked egg recipe

USE THE
METAL BLADE

Remove the bacon rinds and roughly chop the rashers. Place the bacon in the Magimix bowl and process until the bacon is finely chopped. Fry the bacon, without extra fat, over a medium high heat until it is crisp. Drain the bacon pieces and keep warm.

Make the baked eggs exactly as in the basic recipe. As soon as the eggs are cooked, scatter over the cooked, chopped bacon and serve at once.

Baked eggs with tomatoes

Serves 4

1 small bunch chives
2 tomatoes
salt and freshly ground
*   black pepper*

25 g (1 oz) butter
4 tablespoons cream
4 eggs

Roughly chop the chives. Cover the tomatoes with boiling water and leave to stand for 2 minutes. Drain, slide off the tomato skins and cut the tomatoes in half. Remove the core and seeds with a teaspoon.

USE THE
METAL BLADE

Place the chives in the Magimix bowl and process until the chives are finely chopped. Add the tomato halves and process until the tomatoes are finely chopped. Season with salt and pepper and switch on and off to mix the ingredients.

Melt the butter in a saucepan. Add the chives and tomatoes and cook over a medium heat, stirring, for 3 minutes. Divide the mixture between four ramekin dishes. Break in one egg to each ramekin dish and bake in a moderate oven (180°C, 350°F, Reg. 4) for about 8 minutes until just set. Spoon over the cream and serve at once.

Ham and tomato baked eggs

Serves 4

50 g (2 oz) cooked ham	*salt and freshly ground*
2 tomatoes	*black pepper*
25 g (1 oz) butter	*4 eggs*
	4 tablespoons cream

Roughly chop the ham. Cover the tomatoes with boiling water and leave to stand for 2 minutes. Drain well, slide off the tomato skins and halve the tomatoes. With a teaspoon scrape out the tomato cores and seeds.

USE THE
METAL BLADE

Combine the ham and tomatoes and process until the ham is finely chopped.

Melt the butter in a saucepan, add the ham and tomatoes, season with salt and pepper and cook over a medium heat for 2 minutes. Divide the mixture between four ramekin dishes, break over four eggs and bake in a moderate oven (180°C, 350°F, Reg. 4) for about 8 minutes until the eggs are just set.

Pour over the cream and serve at once.

Devilled eggs

Serves 4

There are many variations of devilled eggs and you may well have your own favourite recipe. The same method can be applied in many other recipes.

8 hard-boiled eggs	*salt and freshly ground*
1.5 dl ($\frac{1}{4}$ pint) mayonnaise	*black pepper*
(page 147)	*50 g (2 oz) ham*
2 gherkins	*pinch paprika*
1 teaspoon Dijon mustard	*1 tinned pimento*

USE THE
METAL BLADE

Peel the eggs and cut into halves lengthwise. Carefully remove the yolks. Place the egg yolks in the Magimix

74

bowl with the other ingredients except the pimento. Season with salt, freshly ground black pepper and a pinch of paprika and process until the ingredients are reduced to a paste.

Cut the tinned pimento into thin strips.

Pile the filling into the halved eggs and garnish with crossed strips of pimento.

Note: If you wish to serve the eggs as a salad, arrange them on crisp lettuce leaves and garnish with slices of tomato.

Basque piperade

Serves 6–8

There are many recipes for this delicious mixture of vegetables and eggs. The important thing is not to over-cook the eggs.

1 medium bunch parsley
900 g (2 lb) ripe tomatoes
3 green peppers
2 cloves garlic
1 large onion
6 thin rashers streaky
bacon

3 tablespoons olive or
vegetable oil
salt and freshly ground
black pepper
pinch sugar
6 eggs

Remove the stalks from the parsley. Cover the tomatoes with boiling water for 2 minutes, drain and slide off the tomato skins. Remove the core and seeds of the peppers and roughly chop the flesh. Peel the garlic. Peel and roughly chop the onion. Remove the rinds from the bacon.

USE THE
METAL BLADE

Place the parsley leaves in the Magimix bowl and process until finely chopped. Remove the parsley.

Place the peppers, garlic and onion in the Magimix bowl and process until the ingredients are coarsely chopped.

Heat the oil in a large heavy pan, add the onions, pepper and garlic and cook over a low heat until the onion is soft and transparent.

Place the tomatoes in the Magimix bowl and process until the tomatoes are roughly chopped.

Add the tomatoes to the onion and pepper, season with salt and pepper, add the sugar, cover and cook over a very low heat for about 30 minutes or until most of the liquid has evaporated.

75

Place the eggs in the Magimix bowl and process until just smooth. Add the eggs to the ingredients in the frying pan and cook over a low heat, stirring every now and then, until the eggs are just set. Place the bacon in the Magimix bowl and process until the bacon is finely chopped.

Cook the bacon in a frying pan over a medium high heat until it is crisp. Drain off the fat and stir bacon into the egg mixture. Taste for seasoning, transfer the piperade to a warm serving dish and sprinkle over the parsley.

Serve at once with hot French bread.

Potato and ham cake with fried eggs

Serves 4

1 small onion,
*   peeled and roughly*
*   chopped*
175 g (6 oz) ham
450 g (1 lb) cooked
*   potatoes*

salt and freshly ground
*   black pepper*
3 tablespoons olive oil or
*   vegetable oil*
4 eggs

USE THE
METAL BLADE

Put the onion into the Magimix food processor and process until onion is finely chopped. Remove the onion and put the ham, roughly cut into 2.5 cm (1 in.) cubes, in the bowl and process until ham is finely chopped. Remove ham, put potatoes into Magimix bowl and process until potatoes are smooth. Stop machine, add onions and ham to potato, season with salt and freshly ground black pepper and process for just long enough to mix ingredients.

Heat 2 tablespoons of the oil in an omelette pan. Add the potato mixture pressing it down firmly. Cook over a high heat, scoring through the mixture every now and then to facilitate even cooking, for 20 minutes. Invert the potato cake onto a serving dish.

Add remaining oil to the pan, break in four eggs and cook over a medium heat until eggs are just set. Slide the eggs on top of the potato cake and serve at once.

Making soufflés with your Magimix

Because your Magimix food processor is such a strong machine it is unsuited to whipping egg whites to the point when they will stand in stiff peaks. When making soufflés whip your egg whites separately and process the remaining ingredients in your Magimix food processor to make the best and lightest soufflés you have ever produced.

Make your white sauce base. Chop, grate or purée the ingredients for your soufflé in the Magimix food processor, add the white sauce and process until smooth. Add the egg yolks, one by one, through the feed tube with the machine switched on and season to taste. Add one-third of the stiffly beaten egg whites to the ingredients in the Magimix and switch on and off once or twice to incorporate the egg whites lightly into the soufflé base. Add the ingredients from the Magimix bowl to the remaining stiffly beaten egg whites.

Half fill a well buttered soufflé dish with your mixture and bake it in a hot oven (200°C, 400°F, Reg. 6) for about 25 minutes until well risen.

Rabbit soufflé

Serves 6

50 g (2 oz) butter
50 g (2 oz) flour
3 dl ($\frac{1}{2}$ pint) milk
175 g (6 oz) raw rabbit

2 eggs, separated
salt and freshly ground
black pepper

Melt the butter in a saucepan, add the flour and mix well Gradually add the milk, stirring continually until the sauce comes to the boil and is thick and smooth.

USE THE
METAL BLADE

Place the rabbit meat in the Magimix bowl and process until the rabbit is reduced to a paste. Add the egg yolks and process until the mixture is smooth. Add the white sauce, season and process until smooth.

Whip the egg whites until stiff. Add one third of the egg whites to the ingredients in the Magimix bowl and switch on and off once or twice to incorporate the egg white lightly into the soufflé base. Scrape out the rabbit mixture and fold it lightly into the remaining egg whites.

Turn the mixture in a well buttered soufflé dish and bake in a hot oven (200°C, 400°F, Reg. 6) for 25 minutes until well risen.

Soufflé roulade

Serves 6

This is a most dramatic dish to serve when you want to impress. It isn't, surprisingly, nearly as difficult as it looks and the effect is not only attractive to look at but delicious to eat. A roulade also, unlike a soufflé, keeps warm without losing its lightness and I find them delicious to eat cold too. Prepare the filling in advance – see below.

100 g (4 oz) butter	*4 eggs, separated*
112 g (4½ oz) flour	*salt and cayenne pepper*
6 dl (1 pint) hot milk	*1 tablespoon cream*

Well grease a Swiss roll pan and line it with greaseproof paper leaving an overlap of 4 cm (1½ in.) on each end. Very generously butter the greaseproof paper.

Melt the butter in a saucepan, add the flour and mix well. Gradually blend in the hot milk, stirring continually over a medium high heat until the mixture comes to the boil and is thick and smooth. Simmer for 3 minutes stirring continually. Leave to cool.

USE THE
METAL BLADE

Place the egg yolks in the Magimix bowl and process until smooth. Add the cooled sauce, season with salt and cayenne, add the cream and process until well mixed.

Beat the egg whites until stiff. Add the egg yolk mixture and fold it in lightly.

Spread the mixture over the greaseproof paper, building it up slightly around the edges. Bake the roulade in a preheated moderate oven (180°C, 350°F, Reg. 4) for 20–25 minutes until risen and golden on the top.

Lay a clean tea towel on a working surface, upturn the pan onto the towel and then gently strip off the greaseproof paper. If the roll is to be served hot, spread over the filling, roll up neatly and wrap in foil if the roll is to be kept warm. Serve as soon as possible, cut into thick slices. If the roulade is to be served cold, leave it to cool before spreading over the filling and rolling up.

Hot fillings for a roulade

1. Add 225 g (8 oz) cooked chicken or ham to 3 dl (½ pint) Béchamel sauce, flavour with finely chopped fresh herbs and season with salt and pepper.

2. Cook 225 g (8 oz) spinach until tender, drain well and chop finely with 225 g (8 oz) cooked chicken and

100 g (4 oz) grated Gruyère cheese. Melt 25 g (1 oz) butter in a saucepan, add the spinach mixture and heat through before spreading over the roulade.

3. Combine 3 dl ($\frac{1}{2}$ pint) Béchamel sauce with 225 g (8 oz) sliced and sautéed mushrooms or other cooked, chopped vegetables and heat through before spreading over the roulade.

4. Mix 3 dl ($\frac{1}{2}$ pint) Béchamel sauce with 225 g ($\frac{1}{2}$ lb) cooked, flaked, smoked haddock.

5. Mix duxelles recipe with 1 tin of drained or 225 g ($\frac{1}{2}$ lb) cooked, flaked salmon.

Cold fillings

1. Mix 3 dl ($\frac{1}{2}$ pint) stiff mayonnaise with chopped lobster meat or prawns.

2. Fill the roulade with a Russian salad.

3. Mix 3 dl ($\frac{1}{2}$ pint) stiff mayonnaise with chopped tomatoes, chopped green peppers and fresh herbs.

Spinach soufflé

Serves 4

175 g (6 oz) spinach
37 g (1$\frac{1}{2}$ oz) Cheddar cheese
25 g (1 oz) Parmesan
  cheese
1 small onion
50 g (2 oz) ham
62 g (2$\frac{1}{4}$ oz) butter
pinch salt

37 g (1$\frac{1}{2}$ oz) flour
3 dl ($\frac{1}{2}$ pint) boiling milk
freshly ground black pepper
pinch cayenne pepper and
  ground nutmeg
4 egg yolks
5 egg whites
pinch cream of tartar

Note on spinach

If you are using fresh spinach, blanch it for 5 minutes in boiling water and then drain thoroughly and chop. If using frozen spinach it should be thawed and then chopped if necessary.

USE THE
METAL BLADE

Break the Cheddar cheese into pieces and process until chopped in small pieces. Remove the Cheddar from the bowl. Break the Parmesan up and process until finely ground. Remove the Parmesan from the bowl.

Butter a 1.5 l, 2$\frac{1}{2}$ pint souffle dish and sprinkle the ground Parmesan around the inside of the dish, shaking it well to distribute the cheese evenly. Preheat the oven to 200°C, 400°F, Reg. 6.

Peel and quarter the onion. Process the onion until finely chopped. Remove the onion. Roughly chop the ham and process until well chopped. Remove the ham from the bowl. Melt 12 g ($\frac{1}{2}$ oz) butter in a saucepan and cook the onion and ham for 3 minutes over a low heat.

Turn the heat up under the saucepan to medium high and add the spinach and a pinch of salt. Stir the mixture until as much moisture as possible has been evaporated and the spinach is nearly dry. This will take longer if you use frozen spinach. Remove the pan from the heat.

Melt 50 g (2 oz) butter in another pan and stir in the flour. Cook for about 2 minutes but do not let it brown. Transfer the roux to the Magimix bowl and add the boiling milk, process until smooth. Add a seasoning of salt, pepper, cayenne and nutmeg. With the motor still running, add the egg yolks one at a time allowing each one to be mixed in. Process until well mixed.

Add the egg yolk mixture to the spinach and mix well.

Beat the egg whites with a pinch of salt. When the eggs are foaming, add a pinch of cream of tartar and continue beating until the egg whites are really stiff.

Stir a quarter of the egg whites into the spinach mixture. Add all but a tablespoon of the grated cheese and mix well. Carefully fold in the remainder of the egg whites, turning the mixture over lightly.

Turn the mixture into the prepared soufflé dish and sprinkle the remaining cheese on top. Place the dish in the centre of the preheated oven and turn the heat down to 190°C, 375°F, Reg. 5 and cook the soufflé for 25 to 30 minutes.

Serve at once.

Savoury cheese soufflé

Serves 4

1 tablespoon finely grated Parmesan cheese
100 g (4 oz) Cheddar cheese
50 g (2 oz) butter
37 g (1$\frac{1}{2}$ oz) flour
3 dl ($\frac{1}{2}$ pint) milk
$\frac{1}{2}$ teaspoon celery salt

3 sage leaves
freshly ground black pepper
pinch cayenne
4 egg yolks
5 egg whites
pinch salt
pinch of cream of tartar

Butter a 1.5 l (2$\frac{1}{2}$ pint) soufflé dish and sprinkle the Parmesan cheese around the inside. Preheat the oven to 200°C, 400°F, Reg. 6.

USE THE
GRATING DISC

Break the Cheddar cheese into pieces and grate through the grating disc. Remove the cheese.

USE THE
METAL BLADE

Melt the butter in a saucepan, add the flour and mix well. Cook the roux over a low heat, stirring occasionally, for 3 minutes. Gradually blend in the milk, stirring over a medium high heat until the sauce is thick and smooth. Transfer the sauce to the Magimix bowl and add the celery salt, sage leaves, a good twisting of freshly ground black pepper and a pinch of cayenne. With the machine running, add the egg yolks, one at a time, through the feed tube and process until the mixture is smooth. Add the grated cheese, reserving one tablespoonful, and process until the cheese is mixed in.

Beat the egg whites until foaming, add a pinch of salt and a pinch of cream of tartar and continue beating until the egg whites are really stiff. Add a quarter of the egg whites to the mixture in the Magimix bowl and switch the machine on and off quickly to mix the ingredients.

Fold the mixture from the Magimix bowl into the remaining egg whites and pour into the prepared soufflé dish. Sprinkle the reserved tablespoon of grated cheese on top and place the dish in the centre of the preheated oven. Turn the heat down to 190°C, 375°F, Reg. 5 and cook for 25 to 30 minutes.

Serve at once.

Ham and spinach soufflé

Serves 4

*225 g (8 oz) frozen
  spinach
42 g (1¾ oz) butter
3 tablespoons flour
3 dl (½ pint) milk
3 eggs, separated*

*100 g (4 oz) cooked ham
25 g (1 oz) finely grated
  Parmesan cheese
salt and freshly ground
  black pepper*

Cook the spinach in a very little boiling water until tender and drain well, pressing out as much liquid as possible.

Melt the butter in a saucepan. Add the flour and mix well. Gradually blend in the milk, stirring continually over a medium high heat until the sauce is thick and smooth.

USE THE
METAL BLADE

Place the sauce in the Magimix bowl and with the machine running, add the egg yolks, one by one, processing until

81

the mixture is smooth. Add the spinach, ham and 12 g ($\frac{1}{2}$ oz) cheese, and season with salt and pepper and continue to process until the ham is very finely chopped.

Whip the egg whites until stiff. Add the ham and spinach mixture and fold it lightly into the egg whites.

Turn the mixture in a well greased soufflé dish, sprinkle over the remaining Parmesan and bake in a hot oven (200°C, 400°F, Reg. 6) for 25–30 minutes until well risen and golden brown.

Basic omelette

Serves 2

The art of making the perfect omelette is an art indeed. The great chefs, apparently, shake the eggs to mix them rather than beating them; with the Magimix food processor this process is done by switching the machine on and off and that is enough to mix the eggs without beating them and thereby destroying the texture of the omelette.

6 eggs　　　　　　　　*12 g ($\frac{1}{2}$ oz) butter*
salt and white pepper

USE THE
METAL BLADE

Place the eggs in the Magimix bowl and season with a little salt and pepper. Switch the machine on and turn it off at once.

Melt the butter in a 25 cm (10 in.) omelette pan. As soon as the butter froths but before it begins to colour, add the eggs and swirl them around the pan. Cook over a medium high heat, tilting the pan so that the runny egg from the top runs underneath the mixture that is beginning to set, and cook until the mixture is just on the point of setting–it should be slightly liquid on the top. Slide the omelette from the pan onto a heated serving dish, folding it in half as you do so.

Herb omelette

Serves 2

1 small bunch parsley or　　*basic omelette mixture*
　chervil and chives

USE THE
METAL BLADE

Remove the tough stalks from the parsley or chervil and roughly chop the chives.

Combine the parsley or chervil leaves and the chives in the Magimix bowl and process until the herbs are finely chopped. Add the eggs and proceed exactly as in the recipe for a basic omelette.

Cheese omelette

Serves 2

*37 g (1½ oz) Cheddar
    cheese*

basic omelette mixture

USE THE
METAL BLADE

Place the cheese in the Magimix bowl and process until the cheese is reduced to very fine crumbs. Add the eggs and seasoning and proceed exactly as in the recipe for a basic omelette.

Spinach and smoked salmon omelette

An omelette for a special occasion. Very rich and rare.

Serves 2

*175 g (6 oz) frozen
    spinach
50 g (2 oz) smoked
    salmon pieces
salt, pepper and a pinch
    of nutmeg*

*12 g (½ oz) butter
3 tablespoons cream
Basic omelette recipe*

Cook the spinach in a little boiling water until tender. Drain really well pressing out all excess moisture.
Roughly chop the smoked salmon.

USE THE
METAL BLADE

Place the spinach and smoked salmon in the Magimix bowl and season with salt, freshly ground black pepper and a pinch of nutmeg. Process until the spinach and smoked salmon are finely chopped.
Melt the butter in a saucepan. Add the spinach mixture and heat through. Stir in the cream and keep warm.
Make the omelette in exactly the same way as in the basic omelette recipe and when it is just cooked, spread over the spinach mixture, fold over and slide onto a warm serving dish.

Ham omelette

Serves 2

*50 g (2 oz) ham
2 spring onions
25 g (1 oz) butter
1 tablespoon cream*

*salt and freshly ground
    black pepper
basic omelette recipe*

Roughly chop the ham. Trim and roughly chop the spring onions.

USE THE
METAL BLADE Place the spring onions in the Magimix bowl and process until they are finely chopped. Add the ham and continue to cook until the ham is finely chopped. Stir in the cream, season with salt and pepper and keep warm.

Make the omelette exactly as it is in the basic omelette recipe. As soon as it is cooked, spread over the ham mixture, fold over and slide onto a warm serving dish.

Asparagus omelette

Serves 2

*1 small tin of asparagus
  tips
salt and freshly ground
  black pepper*

*2 tablespoons double cream
25 g (1 oz) butter
basic omelette recipe*

Drain the asparagus tips, season with salt and pepper and add the cream. Melt the butter in a saucepan, add the asparagus mixture, heat through and keep warm.

Make the omelette exactly as in the recipe for the basic omelette and as soon as it is cooked spread over the asparagus cream mixture, fold in half and slide onto a warm serving dish.

Mushroom omelette

Serves 2–3

*2 sprigs parsley
6 eggs
salt and white pepper
100 g (4 oz) firm button
  mushrooms*

*50 g (2 oz) butter
pinch nutmeg
1 tablespoon flour
2 tablespoons cream*

Remove the tough stalks from the parsley.

USE THE
METAL BLADE Place the parsley leaves in the Magimix bowl and process until the leaves are finely chopped. Remove the chopped parsley.

Place the eggs in the Magimix bowl and season with salt and white pepper. Turn the machine on and turn it off at once to break up the eggs. Remove the eggs.

Place the mushrooms in the Magimix bowl and process until the mushrooms are finely chopped.

Melt half the butter in a saucepan. Add the mushrooms and cook over a low heat for 2 minutes. Season with salt, pepper and a pinch nutmeg. Stir in the flour, cook for 1 minute, stirring, and gradually blend in the cream. Remove from the heat and keep warm.

Heat the remaining butter in a 25 cm (10 in.) omelette pan. As soon as the butter is foaming but before it begins to brown, add the eggs, swirling them around the pan. As soon as the bottom of the egg mixture begins to cook, spread the mushroom sauce over the top. Cook over a medium heat until the omelette is just set with the top still remaining a little creamy, fold in half and slide onto a warm serving dish. Sprinkle over the finely chopped parsley and serve at once.

Omelette Arnold Bennett

One of the most simple and yet sophisticated dishes of all times and certainly a king amongst omelette recipes. It must be served as soon as it is cooked.

1 small onion
3 dl ($\frac{1}{2}$ pint) milk
100 g (4 oz) smoked haddock (ask for haddock and do not accept cod)
37 g (1$\frac{1}{2}$ oz) fresh Parmesan

3 eggs, separated
1.5 dl ($\frac{1}{4}$ pint) double cream
50 g (2 oz) butter
salt and white pepper

Peel the onion and place it in a saucepan with the milk. Bring the milk to simmering point, add the haddock and simmer over a low heat until the fish will flake from the bone – about 10 minutes. Drain the haddock and flake the flesh with a fork. Remove any rind from the Parmesan and break the cheese into pieces.

USE THE
METAL BLADE

Put the cheese into the Magimix and process until the cheese is powdered. Remove half the cheese and set aside.

Add the egg yolks to the cheese in the Magimix bowl with one tablespoon of cream and a light seasoning of salt and pepper. Process until lightly mixed.

Put the flaked haddock into a saucepan with half the butter and 3 tablespoons of cream. Cook over a high heat, shaking the pan, until the butter melts. Remove the pan from the heat at once and leave to cool.

Add the fish to the ingredients in the Magimix bowl and switch on and off so that the fish is just mixed. Pour into a bowl. Beat the egg whites until stiff and fold them lightly into the fish mixture with a fork.

85

Melt the remaining butter in an omelette pan until foaming. Add the omelette mixture and cook over a moderately high heat, scoring through with a knife every now and then to encourage even cooking until omelette is just set. Slide onto a heated fireproof serving dish without folding over, sprinkle with the remaining cheese and pour over any remaining cream.

Put under a hot grill for just long enough for the top to be bubbling and lightly browned.

Spanish omelette

Serves 4

75 g (3 oz) lean ham
1 Spanish onion
5 tablespoons olive oil
3 medium potatoes

salt and freshly ground
black pepper
5 eggs

USE THE
METAL BLADE

Process the ham until reduced to the size of peas. Remove the ham.

USE THE
SLICING DISC

Peel and quarter the onion. Slice the onion through the slicing disc and remove from the bowl.

Heat the oil in a frying pan and add the ham and the onion. Cook over a low heat for 2 minutes. Peel the potatoes and slice them through the slicing disc. Add the sliced potatoes to the onions in the frying pan. Season well with salt and freshly ground black pepper, put a lid on the frying pan and cook over a low heat for about 10 minutes until the potato is soft. Drain off any surplus liquid from the pan.

USE THE
PLASTIC BLADE

Break the eggs into the Magimix bowl and turn the machine on and off until the eggs are broken up.

Pour the eggs over the ingredients in the frying pan and stir gently. Cook over a medium heat until the eggs are lightly set. Put the pan under a hot grill until the top is brown and bubbling, slide onto a warm serving dish and serve at once, cut into wedge-shaped pieces.

Meat, poultry, game and pasta dishes

Notes on chopping, mincing or grinding meat

Remember that the Magimix food processor is an extremely strong machine and be careful not to over-process. Recipes indicate whether meat is to be coarsely or finely chopped, or ground.

Remove any tough fibres and gristle before processing the meat. Cut the meat into 2.5 cm (1 in.) cubes.

Do not try to process too much meat at one time

The Magimix is so speedy that two or three quantities of meat can be processed in no time at all but overloading the machine can result in an uneven texture.

Because the Magimix does such a remarkable job of processing meat it is quite possible to utilize the cheaper cuts of meat for such dishes as hamburgers and meat loaves. Use a percentage of fat to lean meat and chop or grind the meat fairly finely to soften the fibrous texture and tenderize the meat.

When you mince meat with a hand mincer you tend to squeeze out a lot of the juice from the meat. In the Magimix food processor all the juice is retained and you may find that you need to use less binding.

Do not add salt to minced meat before frying it as this draws out the juices. Season with salt after the meat has been fried or partially fried.

Ham loaf with herbs

Serves 4–5

A useful way of stretching ham for a picnic or summer buffet party. The ham has a rich, herby flavour and should be cut into very thin slices.

450 g (1 lb) cooked ham	*1 tablespoon savory leaves*
100 g (4 oz) cooked ham fat	*6 juniper berries*
	2 eggs
3 sprigs parsley	*¼ teaspoon ground mace*
1 tablespoon fresh majoram leaves	

Roughly chop the ham. Remove the stalks from the parsley.

USE THE
METAL BLADE

Combine the parsley leaves, majoram and savory leaves in the Magimix bowl and process until the herbs are finely chopped. Add the juniper berries and process until the berries are chopped. Add the eggs and mace and process until the eggs are smoothly beaten. Add the ham and ham fat and process, switching on and off to lightly mix the ingredients.

Pack the meat firmly into an earthenware terrine and set it in a roasting tin filled with enough hot water to come half way up the sides of the terrine. Bake in a moderate oven (180°C, 350°F, Reg. 4) for 1 hour.

Remove the terrine from the water, weight it down (see note on pâtés on page 39) and leave to cool. Refrigerate overnight, turn out and cut into thin slices to serve.

A special fricassee of rabbit and ham

A sauce made in the Magimix food processor completes this simple dish and turns it into a culinary dish of some considerable merit. Serve it on a bed of rice or in a ring of puréed potatoes.

Soak wild rabbit in cold water for 6–8 hours before jointing.

Serves 6

1 small rabbit or 6 rabbit
    joints
seasoned flour
450 g (1 lb) piece of lean
    gammon
4 sticks celery
2 onions
2 carrots

2 tablespoons olive or
    vegetable oil
1 bunch parsley
2 tablespoons flour
2 egg yolks
1 tablespoon dry vermouth
    or dry sherry
3 tablespoons yoghurt
salt and pepper

Joint the rabbit. Coat the joints in seasoned flour. Cut the gammon into 1 cm ($\frac{1}{2}$ in.) dice. Roughly chop the celery. Peel and roughly chop the onions. Peel and roughly chop the carrots.

Heat the oil in a large, heavy pan. Add the vegetables and cook over a low heat until the onion is soft and transparent. Remove the vegetables with a slotted spoon, add the rabbit to the juices in the pan and cook over a high heat until the rabbit is lightly browned on all sides. Add the vegetables and gammon and cover the ingredients with cold water. Bring to the boil, cover tightly and simmer over a low heat for about 1 hour until the rabbit and gammon are tender.

Strain off the stock.

USE THE
METAL BLADE

Put the parsley into the Magimix bowl and process until the leaves and stalks are finely chopped. Add 2 tablespoons flour, the egg yolks, vermouth or sherry and the yoghurt and process until the ingredients are well mixed. With the machine running, pour in 3 dl ($\frac{1}{2}$ pint) stock and process until the ingredients are well mixed.

Turn the ingredients from the Magimix bowl into a clean saucepan. Add another 6 dl (1 pint) of stock and cook over a low heat, stirring all the time, until the sauce thickens to the consistency of thick cream.

Remove the rabbit meat from the bones.

Add the rabbit, gammon and vegetables to the sauce, season with salt and pepper and heat through before serving.

Smothered lamb

Serves 6–8

A really well flavoured dish that transforms a shoulder of lamb into something special.

1 shoulder of lamb
2 tablespoons mint jelly
2 teaspoons dry English mustard
1 egg yolk
2 tablespoons cider vinegar
12 g (½ oz) butter

salt and freshly ground black pepper
2 tablespoons flour
2 teaspoons cornflour
3 dl (½ pint) stock
few drops Angostura bitters

Ask your butcher to bone and trim the meat.

USE THE
METAL BLADE

Combine the mint jelly, mustard, egg yolk, vinegar, and butter in the Magimix bowl and season with salt and black pepper. Process until they are well mixed.

Transfer the mixture to a double boiler and cook over hot water, stirring continually, until the sauce thickens.

Brush the thickened sauce over the lamb and sprinkle over the flour. Roast in a moderately hot oven (200°C, 400°F, Reg. 6), uncovered for 1 hour. Cover with foil or the top of a roasting tin and cook for a further 1 hour. Remove the meat from the pan onto a heated serving dish and keep warm. Pour off the excess fat from the juices in the pan and mix in the cornflour to the juices over a moderate heat. Stir in the remaining vinegar and the stock, bring to the boil, stir until thickened, add a dash of Angostura, check seasoning and strain through a fine sieve.

Lamb Wellington

Serves 6–8

A real gourmet dish for a special occasion. Use your Magimix food processor to make a stuffing that would otherwise entail a lengthened preparation time.

small leg of lamb
1 small bunch parsley
2 onions
2 lamb's kidneys
37 g (1½ oz) butter
225 g (8 oz) firm button mushrooms

pinch thyme and tarragon
salt and freshly ground black pepper
3 tablespoons dry sherry
675 g (1½ lb) puff pastry
1 egg

Ask your butcher to bone the lamb.

Place the parsley in the Magimix bowl and process until finely chopped. Remove the parsley.

Peel and quarter the onion. Remove the skins of the kidneys, cut into quarters and cut out the hard core. Place the onions and kidneys in the Magimix bowl and process until the onions and kidneys are finely chopped. Remove onions and kidneys.

Melt the butter in a frying pan. Add the onions and kidneys and cook over a low heat for 3 minutes, stirring to prevent sticking.

Place the mushrooms in the Magimix bowl and process until mushrooms are finely chopped. Add the mushrooms to the onions and kidneys and cook for 2 minutes. Mix in parsley, thyme and tarragon, season with salt and freshly ground black pepper and blend in the sherry. Stuff the boned leg with half the stuffing mixture and roast the leg in a moderate oven (180°C, 350°F, Reg. 4) for 1 hour.

Roll out the pastry to 3 mm ($\frac{1}{8}$ in.) thickness and spread it with the remaining stuffing. Working quickly so that the pastry does not become too warm, enclose the leg in the pastry, dampening the edges and sealing them tightly together. Brush the pastry with beaten egg and bake in a hot oven (220°C, 425°F, Reg. 7) for 30 minutes.

Carve in the same way as you would an unboned lamb and accompany with gravy, red currant jelly and mint sauce.

Mousse de volaille

Serves 4

A delectable chicken mousse made with bacon and a panade of bread and milk. The texture is light and the dish is infinitely versatile. Serve it hot with a tomato sauce (see page 158) or serve it cold masked with a mayonnaise and with colourful mixed salad on the side. The mixture can also be chilled, formed with two spoons into egg shapes and cooked like quenelles (see page 62).

350 g (12 oz) streaky bacon
350 g (12 oz) onions
225 g (8 oz) chicken breast
*37 g (1½ oz) white bread
    with crusts removed*
3 dl (½ pint) milk
25 g (1 oz) butter
1 teaspoon salt

*⅛ teaspoon nutmeg
    (ground), allspice and
    white pepper*
1 egg
2 egg whites
*1.5 dl (¼ pint) double
    cream*

91

Remove the rind from the bacon and roughly chop the rashers. Peel and roughly chop the onions. Roughly chop the chicken breast.

USE THE
METAL BLADE Place the bread in the Magimix bowl and process until reduced to fine breadcrumbs.

Combine the bread and milk in a saucepan, bring to the boil and simmer, stirring, until the mixture is thick and creamy. Leave to cool.

USE THE
SLICING DISC Process the onions through the slicing disc. Melt the butter in a frying pan, add the onions and cook over a low heat until the onions are soft and transparent. Leave to cool.

USE THE
METAL BLADE Place the bacon in the Magimix bowl and process until the bacon is reduced to a paste. Remove the bacon.

Place the chicken in the Magimix bowl and process until the chicken is very, very finely chopped. Add the bread mixture and onions, season with salt, pepper and the spices and process until well mixed. Add the egg, egg whites and cream and continue to process until smooth. Add the chicken mixture to the bacon and mix well.

Well grease a 1.8 l (3 pint) loaf tin, pack the mixture in firmly and cover with foil. Place the tin in a baking tin and pour in enough hot water to come half way up the sides of the loaf tin. Bake the mousse in a moderate oven (180°C, 350°F, Reg. 4) for $1\frac{1}{2}$ hours or until a knitting needle or skewer plunged into the centre comes out clean.

Turn out the mousse at once if it is to be served hot and cover with a yoghurt and mushroom, or tomato sauce. If the mousse is to be served cold, leave it to cool in the tin. Chill well, turn out and mask with a plain or flavoured mayonnaise.

Maidenwell stuffed, spiced and buttered chicken

Serves 6

Although I say it myself, this really does make a most excellent chicken dish. The flesh is moist and succulent the stuffing is full of flavour and your normal roast chicken pales in comparison. The use of butter is quite lavish so it's not something you will want to produce every day, but for an occasion when something special is required, then I personally think it is hard to beat.

1 teaspoon rosemary leaves
  (fresh if possible)
175 g (6 oz) butter
½ teaspoon chilli powder
grated rind and juice of ½
  lemon
1 medium to large roasting
  chicken
50 g (2 oz) rice

1 medium onion
½ red pepper
2 sticks celery with the
  leaves
chicken liver, heart and
  gizzard
salt and freshly ground
  black pepper
2 tablespoons sherry

USE THE
METAL BLADE Combine the rosemary leaves, 100 g (4 oz) butter, chilli powder, grated lemon rind and juice in the Magimix bowl and process until the ingredients are well mixed.

Using a small sharp knife, gently remove the skin of the breast of the chicken from the flesh trying not to puncture the skin or tear it. Using a small spatula or your fingers, gently push half the mixture inside the skin smoothing it out along the breast. Rub the remaining butter mixture over the outside of the legs and wings.

Cook the rice in boiling, salted water until tender. Peel and roughly chop the onion. Remove the core and seeds of the red pepper and roughly chop the flesh. Roughly chop the celery. Roughly chop the liver, heart and gizzard of the chicken.

Combine the onion, red pepper, celery and chicken giblets in the Magimix bowl and process until the ingredients are finely chopped.

Melt remaining butter in a frying pan. Add the chopped ingredients and cook over a medium heat until the onion is soft and golden. Add the rice, season with salt and pepper and continue to cook for a further 5 minutes.

Stuff the bird with the rice mixture and place it in a roasting tin. Pour over the sherry and roast in a hot oven (230°C, 450°F, Reg. 8) for 15 minutes then remove, baste well and return to a moderate oven (180°C, 350°F, Reg. 4) for a further 60 minutes, basting every now and then, or until the bird is tender.

Chicken risotto

Serves 6

4 rashers streaky bacon
1 large onion
350 g (12 oz) cooked
  chicken
1 chicken liver
75 g (3 oz) Parmesan
  cheese
100 g (4 oz) butter

1.5 dl ($\frac{1}{4}$ pint) dry white
  wine
1.5 l (2$\frac{1}{2}$ pints) chicken
  stock
salt and freshly ground
  black pepper
575 g (1$\frac{1}{4}$ lb) long grain
  rice

Remove the rinds from the bacon and roughly chop the rashers. Peel and roughly chop the onion. Roughly chop the chicken meat. Finely chop the chicken liver.

USE THE
GRATING DISC

Grate the cheese through the grating disc. Remove the cheese.

USE THE
METAL BLADE

Place the bacon in the Magimix bowl and process until the bacon is finely chopped.

Melt half the butter in a large, flameproof casserole. Add the bacon and cook over a medium heat for 3 minutes.

Place the onion in the Magimix bowl and process until the onion is finely chopped. Add the onion and chicken liver to the bacon and cook over a low heat, stirring to prevent browning, until the onion is soft and transparent. Add the wine and cook until the wine has been absorbed by the ingredients.

Add the rice and stir over a low heat until the rice is transparent.

Add 1.5 dl ($\frac{1}{4}$ pint) stock and continue to cook until the stock is absorbed. Add the remaining stock, 1.5 dl ($\frac{1}{4}$ pint) at a time, cooking each time until the stock has been absorbed. At the end of 20 minutes all the stock should have been used and the rice should be tender with the grains still separate.

Place the chicken in the Magimix bowl and process until the chicken is coarsely chopped. Add the chicken to the risotto, season with salt and freshly ground black pepper, mix well and heat through.

Add the remaining butter and the cheese, mix lightly and leave to stand for 3 minutes before serving.

Mushroom risotto

Serves 6

50 g (2 oz) Parmesan
 cheese
1 small onion
350 g (12 oz) firm button
 mushrooms
100 g (4 oz) butter
2.1 dl ($\frac{1}{3}$ pint) dry white
 wine

575 g (1$\frac{1}{4}$ lb) long grain
 rice
1.6 l (2$\frac{3}{4}$ pints) chicken
 stock
salt and freshly ground
 black pepper

USE THE
GRATING DISC

Grate the Parmesan cheese through the grating disc.
Remove the cheese.

USE THE
SLICING DISC

Peel the onion and slice it thinly through the slicing disc.
Remove the onion. Slice the mushrooms through the
slicing disc.

Melt half the butter in a large heavy flameproof
casserole. Add the onion and cook over a low heat,
without browning, until the onion is soft and transparent.
Add the mushrooms and mix well. Pour over the wine
and cook over a low heat until the wine has been absorbed
into the mushrooms and onions. Add the rice and mix
lightly. Cook until the rice has become transparent and
stir in 1.5 dl ($\frac{1}{4}$ pint) stock.

Cook over a medium heat until the liquid has been
absorbed, stirring gently occasionally, and add the remaining stock 1.5 dl ($\frac{1}{4}$ pint) at a time, cooking each time until
the liquid has been absorbed. By the end of 20 minutes
the stock should all have been absorbed and the rice
should be tender with the grains still separate.

Add the remaining butter and the cheese, season with
salt and freshly ground black pepper and mix lightly
before serving.

Cabbage leaves stuffed with lamb

Serves 4–6

450 g (1 lb) lamb
12 large cabbage leaves
1 onion
100 g (4 oz) long grain rice
small bunch mint

salt and freshly ground
 black pepper
3 dl ($\frac{1}{2}$ pint) tomato juice
12 g ($\frac{1}{2}$ oz) butter

USE THE
METAL BLADE

Roughly chop the meat. Cut the hard stalk from the
cabbage leaves and cook the leaves in boiling salted water

until just soft. Drain well. Peel and quarter the onion. Cook the rice in boiling, salted water until tender and drain well.

USE THE
METAL BLADE Place the mint leaves in the Magimix bowl and process until the leaves are finely chopped. Remove the mint, add the onion and process until the onion is finely chopped. Remove the onion from the bowl with the plastic spatula.

Place the meat in the Magimix bowl and process until very finely chopped (this may have to be done in two steps).

Lightly fry the onion in the butter until it is soft and transparent. Combine the mint, onion, meat and rice in a bowl. Season with salt and pepper. Divide the filling between the cabbage leaves and roll them into neat parcels.

Place the rolls in a lightly greased baking dish, pour over the tomato juice, cover with foil and bake in a slow oven (140°C, 275°F, Reg. 1) for $1\frac{1}{2}$ hours.

Serve with mashed potatoes or rice.

Savoury stuffed peppers

Serves 4

Serve this as a main course with mashed potatoes or rice and a vegetable such as ratatouille.

4 large green peppers
450 g (1 lb) pork belly
small bunch chives
1 sprig marjoram or 1.2 ml
  ($\frac{1}{4}$ teaspoon) dried
  marjoram
50 g (2 oz) white bread
  with the crusts removed

2 eggs
salt and freshly ground
  black pepper
pinch nutmeg
100 g (4 oz) Gruyère cheese,
  cut into slices
50 g (2 oz) butter
1.5 dl ($\frac{1}{4}$ pint) stock

Halve the green peppers and remove the seeds and cores. Cut off the rind from the pork and cut the meat into 2.5 cm (1 in.) cubes. Roughly chop the chives. Remove the stalk from the majoram leaves.

USE THE
METAL BLADE Place the chives and marjoram in the Magimix bowl and process until the herbs are finely chopped. Add the bread to the herbs and process until the bread is reduced to coarse crumbs. Add the meat and continue to process until

96

the meat is the consistency of coarse sausage meat. Add the eggs, season with salt, pepper and nutmeg and process until the ingredients are well mixed.

Fill the peppers with the sausage meat mixture and place in a lightly buttered baking dish. Cover with the slices of cheese, dot with butter, pour over the stock and cover lightly with foil. Bake in a moderate oven (180°C, 350°F, Reg. 4) for 45 minutes.

·

Lamb's liver loaf

Serves 4

225 g (8 oz) lamb's liver
1.5 dl (¼ pint) boiling
   water
4 thick slices white bread
1 large onion
25 g (1 oz) butter

100 g (4 oz) fat pork
2 rashers streaky bacon
2 teaspoons lemon juice
1 egg
celery salt and freshly
   ground black pepper

Add the liver to the boiling water and simmer for 2 minutes to firm the meat.

USE THE
METAL BLADE

Remove the crusts from the bread, place the slices in the Magimix bowl and process until reduced to fine breadcrumbs. Remove breadcrumbs.

Peel and quarter the onion, place it in the Magimix bowl and process until finely chopped. Remove the onion and cook until soft and transparent in the butter.

Roughly chop the pork (remove the rind if necessary). Remove the rinds from the bacon and roughly chop the rashers. Drain and roughly chop the liver. Place the pork in the Magimix bowl with the bacon and process until it is the texture of sausage meat. Add the liver and continue to process until the liver is finely chopped. Add the onion, breadcrumbs, lemon juice and egg to the ingredients in the Magimix bowl, season with celery salt and freshly ground black pepper and process until ingredients are well mixed. Turn into a well greased loaf tin, cover with foil and bake for 1 hour in a moderately hot oven (190°C, 375°F, Reg. 5). Turn out and serve with tomato sauce (see page 158).

Note The loaf can also be used as a sandwich filling or served cold.

97

Hamburgers

The great all-American invention which has been copied by almost every country in the world. With the Magmix food processor you can make your own hamburgers with the best possible results; succulent patties that are full of flavour and can fit any bill from a sophisticated luncheon to a picnic meal.

So often hamburgers are a pale imitation of the real thing. In the commercial products the meat is often inferior, mincing causes a dry uninteresting texture and a high proportion of stretching ingredients destroy the flavour. By using the Magimix food processor to process the meat and any other ingredients the best possible results are obtained resulting in rich and juicy hamburgers full of taste.

If you wish to stretch your meat, you can add breadcrumbs or cooked potato to the mixture and by altering the seasoning and flavour of the hamburgers you can produce some really exciting meals.

If the meat mixture is too dry to shape into patties, add a small egg to the meat in the bowl and process for just long enough to mix the ingredients. With the Magimix food processor it is not necessary to use the most expensive meat for making your hamburgers. I have produced very successful patties from chuck, for instance, but you must take care to remove any gristle before processing the meat. Make sure that the meat you use has a certain amount of fat in it or the hamberger will inevitably tend to be on the dry side.

Basic hamburgers

Serves 4

450 g (1 lb) beef steak   *black pepper*
salt and freshly ground

Remove any gristle and cut the meat into 2.5 cm (1 in.) cubes.

USE THE
METAL BLADE

Place the meat in the Magimix bowl and process until the texture is that of coarsely minced (ground) meat (do not over process as the texture is important). Shape the meat with the hands into four 1 cm ($\frac{1}{2}$ in.) thick patties.

Preheat a large, heavy frying pan until a small piece of meat sizzles when it is dropped into the pan.

Place the patties in the pan and cook over a very high heat for 3 minutes. Turn over, season with salt and pepper and continue to cook until the hamburgers are cooked to the degree you require.

Variations

1. Place a slice of processed Cheddar cheese on top of each hamburger and grill them for a minute or two until the cheese has melted just before serving.

2. For a hot hamburger: add 2 teaspoons chilli sauce, 1 mashed anchovy fillet and 1 teaspoon finely chopped capers to the meat.

3. For herb flavoured hamburgers: finely chop 1 small bunch parsley and chives before adding the meat to the Magimix bowl.

4. The hamburgers can be topped by onions, sliced with the slicing disc and fried until golden brown in butter before the hamburgers are cooked.

5. Hamburgers can be topped with herb or savoury butters, see page 166.

To make a gravy for hamburgers: transfer the cooked hamburgers to a warmed serving dish. Add 1.5 dl ($\frac{1}{4}$ pint) stock to the juices in the pan, bring to the boil, stirring continually over a medium high heat and add a little Worcestershire sauce.

Bifteck haché à la lyonnaise

Serves 4

The Frenchman's answer to the American hamburger and a very good answer it is too; the sauce gives it that essential French 'je ne sais quoi' and makes this kind of burger a dinner party speciality rather than just a quick meal.

675 g (1½ lb) lean beef
1 small onion
1 large egg
salt and freshly ground
* black pepper*

flour
1.5 dl (¼ pint) red wine
42 g (1¾ oz) butter

Remove any gristle from the meat and roughly chop the flesh. Peel and quarter the onion.

USE THE
METAL BLADE

Place one third of the meat in the Magimix bowl and process until the meat has been finely chopped to the

99

consistency of a coarse mince. Remove the meat and process the remaining beef in two more operations. Remove
the meat each time. Place the onion in the Magimix bowl
and process until finely chopped. Add the egg and switch
on and off to beat the egg with the onions. Pour the egg
and onion mixture over the meat, season with salt and
freshly ground black pepper and mix well. Shape into
eight circular cakes 1 cm ($\frac{1}{2}$ in.) thick, cover with foil and
place in the refrigerator for 1 hour.

Lightly coat the *Biftecks* with flour and fry in hot oil for
3 minutes each side. Drain on kitchen paper, transfer to
a serving dish and keep warm.

Pour the wine into the pan in which the *biftecks* were
cooked, scraping up any sediment sticking to the pan.
Bring to the boil and cook over a high heat, stirring, until
the sauce is slightly thickened and reduced. Remove from
the heat, stir in the butter and spoon some of the sauce
over each of the *biftecks*.

Steak tartare

Serves 4

Mincing ruins both the taste and flavour of this delicious,
sophisticated and nourishing dish. With the Magimix
food processor none of the juice is lost from the meat and
mouth-watering steak tartare can be produced in seconds.

4 sprigs parsley
1 small onion
450 g (1 lb) rump steak
$\frac{1}{2}$ teaspoon Worcestershire
  sauce
1 teaspoon brandy

2 drops Tabasco sauce
$\frac{1}{4}$ teaspoon Dijon mustard
salt and freshly ground
  black pepper
4 eggs
3 tablespoons capers

Remove the stalks from the parsley. Peel and roughly
chop the onion. Cut the meat into 2.5 cm (1 in.) cubes.

Put the parsley leaves in the Magimix bowl and process
until the parsley is finely chopped. Remove the parsley.
Put the onion in the Magimix bowl and process until the
onion is finely chopped. Remove the onion. Put half the
meat in the Magimix bowl and process for just long enough

for it to become the consistency of finely minced (ground) meat. Remove and process the rest of the meat.

Put the meat into a bowl. Add the Worcestershire sauce, brandy, Tabasco and mustard, season with salt and freshly ground black pepper and mix well. Divide the meat onto four plates and shape into mounds. Make a well in the centre of each mound and place a raw egg in each well. Garnish the steak tartare with portions of finely chopped parsley and onions and the capers and chill before serving.

Home made sausages

With a Magimix in your kitchen you can make your own sausages quickly and easily and re-discover the full flavoured taste of sausages as they used to be, succulent, aromatic and bursting with juice as they cook. Sausage skins can be bought from your butcher who will also, for a reasonable sum, fill the skins with your own mixture. A simple sausage skin filling attachment is now on the market at a reasonable price.

Spiced pork sausages

---

450 g (1 lb) lean pork belly
450 g (1 lb) shredded beef suet
pinch dried marjoram, thyme and savory

grated rind of 1 lemon
salt and freshly ground black pepper
$\frac{1}{4}$ teaspoon dried sage
large pinch ground nutmeg
1 egg

Remove the rind from the pork and cut the flesh into 1 inch cubes.

USE THE
METAL BLADE

Place the pork in the Magimix bowl and process until the meat is coarsely ground. Remove two thirds of the pork, add one third of the beef suet, the lemon rind and one third of the herbs and a seasoning of salt and pepper. Process until the ingredients are well mixed and the pork is finely ground. Remove to a large bowl.

Combine half the remaining pork, suet and herbs in the Magimix bowl, season and process as above. Remove to the large bowl and replace with remaining pork, suet and herbs. Season, add the egg and process as above. Combine all the sausage mixture in the large bowl and mix well before filling into skins.

101

Cumberland sausage

Unlike most sausages which are twisted into links, this well flavoured sausage is traditionally made in a long coil and cut into serving portions after it is cooked.

225 g (½ lb) lean pork
150 g (6 oz) pork fat
100 g (4 oz) white
    breadcrumbs

½ teaspoon ground nutmeg
¼ teaspoon ground mace
salt and freshly ground
    black pepper.

USE THE
METAL BLADE

Cut the lean and fat pork into 1 in. cubes.
Combine the pork and fat in the Magimix bowl and process until the meat is coarsely ground. Add the breadcrumbs and spices, season with salt and freshly ground black pepper and process until the ingredients are well mixed and the meat is finely ground.

Force the sausage filling into one continuous skin and tie each end. Form into a coil and boil, fry or grill until tender.

Meat croquettes

Serves 4

A useful way to use up small amounts of leftover meat or poultry. Chill the mixture well before shaping it into the croquettes.

225 g (8 oz cooked meat,
    ham or poultry (or a
    combination of meat or
    poultry and ham)
1 small onion
1 small bunch parsley
50 g (2 oz) Gruyère or
    Cheddar cheese

37 g (1½ oz) butter
2 tablespoons flour
1.5 dl (¼ pint) stock
salt and freshly ground
    black pepper
1 egg
browned breadcrumbs

Cut the meat into 2.5 cm (1 in.) cubes. Peel and roughly chop the onion. Remove the tough stalks from the parsley. Break up the cheese.

USE THE
METAL BLADE

Place the cheese in the Magimix bowl and process until the cheese is finely ground. Remove the cheese.

Place the parsley leaves in the Magimix bowl and process until the leaves are finely chopped. Add the onion to the parsley and process until the onion is coarsely chopped. Add the meat to the ingredients in the bowl and process until the meat is coarsely chopped.

Melt the butter in a saucepan. Add the flour and mix well. Gradually blend in the stock, stirring continually over a medium heat until the mixture is thick and smooth. Add the sauce to the ingredients in the bowl, season with salt and pepper and switch on and off to mix the ingredients – do not over-process.

Turn the mixture into a shallow dish and chill in a refrigerator for at least an hour before shaping.

Divide the mixture into eight pieces and, using floured hands, shape the pieces into neat sausage shapes on a well floured board.

Coat the croquettes in beaten egg and then in breadcrumbs and deep fry in hot fat or oil for about 5 minutes until golden brown. Drain on kitchen paper and serve as soon as possible.

Brasciolette

Serves 4

small bunch parsley, stalks removed
350 g (12 oz) shin beef
2 pieces white bread
4 tablespoons stock (or use $\frac{1}{2}$ stock cube in water)

salt and freshly ground black pepper
450 g (1 lb) topside
4 rashers bacon with the rinds removed

USE THE
METAL BLADE

Place the parsley in the Magimix bowl and process for a few seconds until parsley is finely chopped. Remove the parsley.

Trim excess fat and any gristle off the shin and cut it into rough chunks. Put about a quarter of the shin into the Magimix bowl with the two slices of bread, broken up, and turn the machine on. With the machine running, drop the remainder of the shin, a few pieces at a time, through the feed tube. Process until the meat is very finely chopped. Stop the machine, add the chopped parsley and stock, season well with salt and freshly ground black pepper and process until the ingredients are well mixed.

Cut the topside into eight slices about 4 cm (1$\frac{1}{2}$ in.) wide and 10 cm (4 in.) long. Beat or roll the slices until they are very thin. Divide the bacon rashers into two and lay a half a rasher on each slice of topside. Season with a little salt and plenty of freshly ground black pepper. Divide the filling into eight portions and place a portion on top of each slice. Roll up the slices firmly into neat parcels and place side by side in a shallow greased fireproof dish. Cover the rolls with foil and cook in a very moderate oven (170°C, 325°F, Reg. 3) for $1\frac{1}{2}$ hours.

Serve with a tomato sauce (page 158).

Beef loaf

Serves 6–8

2 slices white bread
450 g (1 lb) lean chuck
  steak
225 g ($\frac{1}{2}$ lb) lean ham

good pinch nutmeg
5 ml (1 teaspoon) salt
freshly ground black pepper
1 egg

USE THE
METAL BLADE

Remove the crusts from the bread. Process slices in the Magimix food processor until they are reduced to coarse breadcrumbs. Remove the breadcrumbs.

Cut the beef into 2.5 cm (1 in.) cubes removing any gristle. Chop the ham into rough chunks. Process the ham in the Magimix for a few seconds until it is coarsely minced. Remove the ham. Process the beef in the Magimix in two batches, switching the machine on and off frequently until the beef is coarsely minced.

Place the breadcrumbs, ham, beef, nutmeg, salt and freshly ground black pepper into a large bowl. Lightly beat the egg and pour it into the mixture. Stir the mixture well until the ingredients are amalgamated. Pour the mixture into a greased 1.2 l (2 pint) pudding basin, packing it down firmly. Cover tightly with a piece of buttered foil.

Pour enough cold water into a large saucepan to come half to three-quarters of the way up the side of the basin. Place the basin in the saucepan and bring to the boil over a high heat. Cover the pan tightly and simmer for 2 hours. Check the water level now and then to make sure it does not boil dry.

Remove the basin from the saucepan and take off the foil. Cover the beef loaf with a clean piece of foil and put a plate on top of the basin. Weight the plate down with a heavy pan or casserole and leave to cool. With the weight still in place, move the basin to a refrigerator and leave for a further 5 hours.

Dip the basin in boiling water for a few seconds and run a sharp knife around the sides. Turn the beef loaf out on to a plate and serve with mustard and French bread.

104

Braised rump steak with wine and tomatoes

Serves 6

For special occasions one sometimes wants to provide the best, steak for instance, without wanting to spend most of the dinner party cooking it at the last moment. This classic way of cooking rump steak provides the best of both worlds. It is left to cook by itself with the juices amalgamating to produce a delicious sauce and yet the flavour and tenderness of the meat is unimpaired by the long cooking process.

1 large clove garlic
900 g (2 lb) rump steak
cut into 6 slices
1 large onion
2 medium carrots
450 g (1 lb) ripe tomatoes
2 tablespoons vegetable oil
6 tablespoons dry white wine

2 tablespoons medium dry sherry
2 tablespoons brandy
salt and freshly ground black pepper
1½ tablespoons finely chopped parsley

Peel and halve the garlic and rub the slices of rump on both sides with the cut garlic clove. Peel the onion and clean the carrots.

USE THE
SLICING DISC

Slice the onions and carrots through the slicing disc. Remove the onion and carrots.

USE THE
METAL BLADE

Peel the tomatoes by pouring boiling water over them, leaving the tomatoes to stand for 2 minutes, draining them and then sliding off the skins.

Roughly chop the tomatoes, place them in the Magimix bowl and process until they are finely chopped.

Heat the oil in a large heavy flame proof casserole. Add the meat and cook very quickly over a high heat to brown and seal the meat on both sides. Remove the steaks, add the onions and carrots to the juices in the pan and cook over a medium heat until onions are golden brown.

Arrange the steaks over the vegetables, pour in the wine, sherry and brandy, season with salt and freshly ground black pepper and simmer for 2 minutes. Spread the tomatoes over the meat, season them also with a little salt and pepper and cover the casserole tightly using a sheet of foil under the lid if necessary. Cook in the centre of a slow oven (150°C, 300°F, Reg. 2) for 2 hours. Sprinkle with parsley and serve with puréed potatoes.

105

Cottage pie

Serves 4

One of the best or worst of British main course dishes Cottage Pie is all too often ruined by over-mincing which squeezes out the juices from the cooked meat. With the Magimix food processor however all the flavour and goodness of the meat and vegetables are retained and your leftover beef or lamb is used to its greatest advantage.

1 large onion
1 carrot
450 g (1 lb) lean cooked
  beef or lamb
675 g (1½ lb) cooked
  potatoes
2 tablespoons milk
25 g (1 oz) butter

salt and freshly ground
  black pepper
1½ tablespoons dripping
1 tablespoon flour
2 tablespoons tomato
  purée
pinch mixed herbs
3 dl (½ pint) stock

Peel and roughly chop the onion. Peel and roughly chop the carrot. Cut the meat into 2.5 cm (1 in.) cubes.

USE THE
METAL BLADE

Place the potatoes in the Magimix bowl with the milk and butter. Season with salt and freshly ground black pepper and process until the potatoes are smooth and puréed. Remove the potatoes.

Place the carrot in the Magimix bowl and process until coarsely chopped. Add the onion and continue to process until the onion is finely chopped. Remove the carrot and onion.

Place the meat in the Magimix bowl and process until the meat is the consistency of minced meat.

Heat the dripping. Add the carrot and onion and cook over a low heat until the onion is soft and transparent. Raise the heat, add the meat and cook over a high heat, stirring, until the meat is well browned. Stir in the flour and mix well. Blend in the tomato purée, add the herbs and gradually mix in the stock, stirring continually over a medium high heat until the ingredients come to the boil. Season with salt and freshly ground black pepper, cover and simmer gently for 30 minutes.

Turn the meat into a baking dish and top with the mashed potato. Decorate with a pattern made with the back of a fork and bake in a moderately hot oven (190°C, 375°F, Reg. 5) for 20–30 minutes until the topping is crisp and golden brown.

Galettes de pommes de terre farcies

Serves 4

An attractive way to use up leftover potatoes and meat, poultry or ham. The filling is sandwiched between layers of puréed potatoes, coated with crisp breadcrumbs and fried until crisp on both sides.

4 spring onions
50 g (2 oz) ham, chicken
*   or cooked meat*
450 (1 lb) boiled potatoes
3 egg yolks
37 g (1½ oz) melted butter
2 tablespoons double cream

salt, pepper and a pinch of
*   ground nutmeg*
50 g (2 oz) Gruyère cheese
100 g (4 oz) firm button
*   mushrooms*
100 g (4 oz) dry white
*   breadcrumbs*
oil for frying

Trim and roughly chop the spring onions. Roughly chop the ham, chicken or cooked meat.

USE THE
METAL BLADE

Combine the potato, egg yolks, 25 g (1 oz) melted butter and cream in the Magimix bowl and season with salt, pepper and a pinch of nutmeg. Process until the potatoes are reduced to a smooth purée (do not over-process). Remove from the bowl and chill in the refrigerator until required. Wash out the bowl and dry it well.

USE THE
GRATING DISC

Grate the cheese through the grating disc. Remove the cheese.

USE THE
METAL BLADE

Place the spring onions in the Magimix bowl and process until finely chopped. Add the mushrooms to the spring onions and process until the mushrooms are finely chopped.

Heat 12 g (½ oz) melted butter in a frying pan. Add the onions and mushrooms and cook over a low heat until the onions are soft and transparent.

Place the ham, chicken or cooked meat in the Magimix bowl and process until the ham is finely chopped. Add the ham to the onions and mushrooms and continue to cook over a low heat for 2 minutes. Season with salt and pepper.

Shape half the potato mixture into eight flat cakes about 6 mm (¼ in.) thick. Spread with the filling, top with grated cheese and cover with eight more cakes of the same size. Press firmly together and dredge in white breadcrumbs.

Fry the cakes in hot oil for about 4 minutes on each side until crisp and golden brown.

The cakes can also be placed in a greased baking dish, sprinkled with breadcrumbs and with 37 g (1½ oz) melted butter and baked in a hot oven (200°C, 400°F, Reg. 6) for 30 minutes until golden brown.

Sausagemeat stuffing

A traditional must with turkey . . . one end or the other. You can also use it to 'stretch' a chicken into extra servings, roll it into balls and fry them until crisp in fat or dripping to serve with roast chicken or roast pork or use the mixture as a stuffing for green peppers.

1 large onion
2 cloves garlic
2 tablespoons lard or
  dripping
450 g (1 lb) pork belly
  with rind removed
1 small bunch parsley

2 sage leaves
1 small sprig thyme
50 g (2 oz) white bread
  with the crust removed
grated rind of ½ a lemon
salt and freshly ground
  pepper

Peel and quarter the onion. Peel and roughly chop the garlic cloves. Roughly chop the pork. Remove the stalks of the parsley, sage and thyme and roughly chop the bread.

USE THE
METAL BLADE

Place the herbs in the Magimix bowl and process until the herbs are finely chopped. Add the bread and process until the bread is reduced to coarse breadcrumbs. Remove the herbs and bread.

Place the pork in the Magimix bowl and process until the pork is very finely chopped. Add the onion and garlic and continue to process until the onion is finely chopped. Add the dripping, bread and herbs and lemon rind, season with salt and pepper and process for just long enough for the ingredients to become well mixed.

108

English sage and onion stuffing

Use for stuffing a boned leg or shoulder of pork or form it into small balls and fry them in fat or dripping to go with a joint of roast pork on the bone.

4 onions
225 g (8 oz) white bread
with the crusts removed
8 sage leaves

37 g (1½ oz) butter, melted
salt and white pepper
1 small egg, beaten

Peel and quarter the onions. Roughly chop the bread.

USE THE
METAL BLADE Place the sage leaves in the Magimix bowl and process until finely chopped. Add the bread to the sage and process until the bread is reduced to coarse breadcrumbs. Add the melted butter, season with salt and white pepper and process until well mixed. With the machine switched on, add enough beaten egg through the feed tube to bind the ingredients.

Chestnut stuffing

Enough to stuff a 4.5 kg (10 lb) turkey.

450 g (1 lb) fresh chestnuts
3 dl (½ pint) milk
1 onion
50 g (2 oz) bacon
3 sprigs parsley
100 g (4 oz) white bread
with the crusts removed

25 g (1 oz) butter
finely grated rind of 1
lemon
1 egg
salt and freshly ground
black pepper

Cut a cross on the top of each chestnut. Place them in boiling water, return to the boil and cook for 5 minutes to soften the skins. Drain, leave until cool enough to handle and remove the shells and the brown skin of the nuts.

Combine the chestnuts and milk in a saucepan, bring to the boil and simmer for 30–40 minutes until the chestnuts are soft.

Peel and quarter the onion. Remove the rinds from the bacon and chop the rashers. Remove the stalks from the parsley.

USE THE
METAL BLADE Place the parsley leaves in the Magimix bowl and process until the leaves are finely chopped. Remove the parsley.

Place the bread in the Magimix bowl and process until it is reduced to coarse breadcrumbs. Remove the bread. Place the bacon in the Magimix bowl and process until the bacon is finely chopped. Remove the bacon. Place the onion in the Magimix bowl and process until finely chopped. Melt the butter in a frying pan. Add the onion and cook over a low heat until the onion is soft and transparent. Add the bacon and continue to cook over a low heat, stirring to prevent sticking, for a further 5 minutes.

Place the chestnuts in the Magimix bowl and process until the chestnuts are puréed. Stop the machine, add the onions, bacon and the juice from the pan, the breadcrumbs, lemon rind and the parsley. Add the egg, season and process for just long enough to incorporate the ingredients.

Marinade for meat

Try marinading lamb or pork chops overnight in this mixture or use it to flavour kebabs that are to be cooked on a barbecue. Enough marinade for eight chops.

1 onion
a piece of ginger root 2.5 cm (1 in.) long
5 cloves garlic
1 small tin tomatoes
1 tablespoon tomato purée
1 tablespoon ground coriander
$\frac{1}{4}$ teaspoon ground cumin
$\frac{1}{2}$ teaspoon ground turmeric
pinch ground mace
pinch ground cloves
salt and freshly ground black pepper
2 tablespoons olive or vegetable oil
$\frac{1}{2}$ teaspoon cayenne pepper
juice of 1 lemon

USE THE
METAL BLADE

Peel and quarter the onion. Peel and chop the ginger root. Peel the garlic cloves. Combine all the ingredients in the Magimix bowl and process until the onion is reduced to a pulp.

Place the meat in a bowl, pour over the marinade and leave to marinate for at least 8 hours.

Fried onion strips

Serves 6
Delicious crisp strips of onion that go well with almost any main course dish. Drain the strips well on kitchen paper to prevent them going soft.

3 largish onions	*salt and freshly ground*
milk	*black pepper*
flour	*oil for frying*

Peel the onions and cut them into pieces just large enough to go through the feed tube.

USE THE
SLICING DISC
Slice the onions through the slicing disc. Place the onions in a shallow dish and cover them with milk. Leave the onions to stand for 30 minutes, drain them well and dip the strips into flour seasoned with salt and freshly ground black pepper. Fry the strips in very hot oil until golden brown and crisp and drain them well on kitchen paper.

Do not fry too many strips at once and keep the cooked strips warm while frying the rest.

Pasta with delicious sauces made in your Magimix food processor

I make a point of visiting Italy at least once a year. Not only do I find great *simpatía* amongst the people I meet there but I find the enjoyment I get from even the most simple of their dishes a fresh joy every time I experience it. Staying there I became a dedicated pasta lover, revelling in their fish dishes and delighted in their lavish use of herbs with roast and grilled meats. It was in Italy that I first learnt to sprinkle grilled meat as well as fish with lemon, to throw herbs on my barbecue before starting to cook and to differentiate between different classes of olive oil.

The sauces for Italian pasta dishes vary enormously from region to region and their variations could, and have, filled many books. Most of them make delicious and economical main courses, those on the lighter side make a perfect start to many a good meal and I find the satisfaction I derive from making them a constant joy to both myself and those who eat at my table.

All the sauces require chopping, grating or slicing in one way or another, some require quite complicated amounts of preparation, but in every sauce you make, the Magimix food processor will cut down your preparation time by at

111

least half, making even the most sophisticated of pasta sauces a quick and easy process. Your sauces will be more successful because the ingredients will be evenly processed and those containing meat will taste twice as good because the meat will be finely chopped rather than being minced or ground.

If you follow the steps for the preparation of these sauces laid out in the following recipes there will be no need to wash out your Magimix bowl in between processing different ingredients.

Macaroni alla siciliana

Serves 6–8

Although many of the traditional Italian pasta dishes are quite complex, the work entailed in the production of the recipe is amply rewarded by the economical and sophisticated result. Most of the preparation involved in making these dishes consists of slicing, chopping and grating and by using your Magimix food processor you can cut the preparation time by at least half. In this dish macaroni is mixed with a fragrant tomato sauce flavoured with basil. The dish is topped with crisply fried aubergine slices and meat balls in miniature.

2 onions
100 g (4 oz) beef rump,
 topside or chuck
4 aubergines
salt
12 leaves basil with the
 · stalks removed
flour
37 g (1¼ oz) lard

1 large tin tomatoes
freshly ground black
 pepper
675 g (1½ lb) macaroni
4 tablespoons olive oil
100 g (4 oz) Cheddar
 cheese or other grating
 cheese

Peel and quarter the onions. Cut the meat into rough pieces discarding any gristle.

USE THE
SLICING DISC

Slice the aubergines, without peeling, through the slicing disc. Arrange the slices on a flat dish, sprinkle with salt and leave to 'sweat' for 20 minutes.

USE THE
METAL BLADE

Place the basil leaves in the Magimix bowl and process until the leaves are finely chopped. Remove the basil.

Place the onions in the Magimix bowl and process until finely chopped. Remove the onions.

112

Place the meat in the Magimix bowl and process until the meat is finely chopped. Dip your hands in flour and shape the meat into tiny balls about the size of large peas. Roll the meat balls in flour.

Melt the lard in a saucepan, add the onions and cook over a low heat until the onion is soft and transparent. Add the tomatoes and basil, season with salt and freshly ground black pepper, bring to the boil, cover and simmer, stirring occasionally for 20 minutes.

Cook the macaroni in plenty of boiling, salted water until just tender. Drain well and reserve a little of the water. Drain off the liquid from the aubergine slices, pat them dry on kitchen paper and coat them with flour.

Heat the oil in a frying pan, add the aubergine slices, a few at a time, and fry over a high heat until crisp and golden brown. Drain well on kitchen paper and keep warm. Add the meat balls to the oil in the pan and cook over a high heat, shaking the pan to prevent burning, until the meat balls are browned on all sides. Remove with a slotted spoon, drain on kitchen paper and keep warm.

Add the macaroni and the grated cheese to the tomato sauce with 2 tablespoons water in which the macaroni was cooked. Mix well until the ingredients are hot and the cheese has melted. Turn the macaroni on to a heated serving dish and top with the aubergine slices and meat balls.

Serve at once with a green or mixed salad.

Spaghetti alla carbonara

Serves 6

One of the simplest but most delicious of spaghetti dishes and a recipe I consider to be one of the best of almost all instant emergency standbys.

175 g (6 oz) streaky bacon	6 eggs
675 g (1½ lb) spaghetti	2 tablespoons double
100 g (4 oz) Parmesan or	(whipping) cream
Pecorino cheese	salt and freshly ground
1 tablespoon olive oil	black pepper

Remove the rinds from the bacon and roughly chop the rashers. Make the sauce while the spaghetti is cooking. Cook the spaghetti in plenty of boiling, salted water until it is just tender.

113

Place the Parmesan cheese in the Magimix bowl and process until the cheese is finely powdered. Remove the cheese.

Put the bacon in the Magimix bowl and process until the bacon is finely chopped.

Heat the oil in a frying pan, add the bacon and cook over a low heat until the bacon fat is transparent.

Break the eggs into the Magimix bowl with the cream and a seasoning of salt and plenty of freshly ground black pepper and process until the eggs are smooth (do not over-process).

Drain the spaghetti and return it to the pan. Add the bacon, the juices in which it was fried and the egg mixture and toss well over a medium heat until the spaghetti is coated with the sauce and the ingredients are hot through – do not allow the sauce to cook. Turn onto a hot serving dish and serve Parmesan cheese on the side.

Tagliatelle with ham and cream sauce

Serves 4

Another of those almost instant dishes which is not only economical but very delicious too. With the Magimix food processor and a quick cooking tagliatelle it can be produced in almost minutes and with a green salad makes a very acceptable main course.

*1 small bunch parsley
  with the stalks removed
1 small onion
2 cloves garlic, peeled
175 g (6 oz) ham
350 g (12 oz) tagliatelle*

*2 tablespoons olive or
  vegetable oil
1.5 dl ($\frac{1}{4}$ pint) cream
freshly ground black
  pepper*

Put the parsley leaves into the Magimix bowl and process until finely chopped. Remove the parsley.

Peel and quarter the onion. Combine the onion and garlic in the Magimix bowl and process until the onion is chopped but not too fine. Add the ham, roughly chopped into 2.5 cm (1 in.) cubes and process until the ham is chopped.

Cook the tagliatelle in boiling, salted water until just tender. Drain well. Heat the oil in a small saucepan, add the onion and garlic and cook over a low heat until onion is soft and transparent. Add the ham and parsley and continue to cook over a low heat for a further two minutes. Mix in the cream and season with freshly ground black pepper (I do not suggest adding salt as the ham is often rather on the salty side itself). Heat through without boiling.

Add the sauce to the tagliatelle in a large saucepan and toss over a low heat until all the ingredients are hot through. Turn into a heated serving dish and serve at once with grated Parmesan cheese on the side.

Spaghetti with an egg and walnut sauce

Serves 6

This makes an excellent dish to serve as a first course on a hot summer evening. It must be served as soon as it is finished but the sauce can be made in advance and the spaghetti, after all, can be left to its own devices provided you do not allow it to overcook.

*100 g (4 oz) Parmesan
  cheese
    Parmesan cheese
225 g (8 oz) shelled
  walnuts
5 medium egg yolks
3 dl (¼ pint) single
  (pouring) cream*

*100 g (4 oz) butter,
  melted
salt and freshly ground
  black pepper
675 g (1½ lb) spaghetti*

USE THE
METAL BLADE

Break the Parmesan up into the bowl and process until the cheese has powdered, add the walnuts and process until the walnuts are roughly chopped. Add the egg yolks, cream and melted butter, season with salt and pepper and continue to process until the walnuts are finely chopped and the eggs are smooth. Do not over-process.

Cook the spaghetti in boiling salted water until just tender. Drain well.

Pour the sauce into a large saucepan, add the spaghetti and toss well until the spaghetti is coated with the sauce and the dish is hot through. Do not overcook, the sauce should be creamy and not like scrambled eggs.

Turn onto a warm serving dish and serve at once.

115

Home-made pasta

Making your own pasta with your Magimix food processor is surprisingly easy and extremely rewarding. Home-made pasta, cooked the day it has been made is far more full of flavour than a commercial product and, indeed, is so delicious in its own right that it merely needs the addition of some butter and Parmesan cheese to embellish the dish.

There are extremely efficient pasta-making machines on the market which will roll and cut the dough into the required thickness.

3 eggs	*1 small teaspoon salt*
450 g (1 lb) plain flour	*1.2 dl (4 fl. oz) water*

USE THE
METAL BLADE Place the eggs in the Magimix bowl. Process until the eggs are thoroughly mixed and then, with the motor running, add the flour through the feed tube with the salt. As soon as the flour has been added, add the water through the feed tube and process until the dough forms a ball around the metal blade. Continue to process for a further 60 seconds to knead the dough. It should be absolutely smooth.

Place the dough on a well floured board and roll it out to paper thin consistency – dust the dough frequently with plain flour (or, even better, with semolina flour which you can buy from a delicatessen specializing in Italian products) and leave to rest for 30 minutes.

LASAGNE

Cut the dough into rectangles about 7.5 cm (3 in.) wide by 15–20 cm (6–8 in.) long. Dust with flour after cutting.

FETTUCINE, TAGLIATELLE AND NOODLES

Dust the dough generously with flour and roll it lightly as you would a pancake. Cut slices from the roll of the thickness you require. Hang the unrolled ribbons of pasta over the back of a chair to dry.

To cook

Drop the pasta into a large pan of fast boiling, salted water and boil for 8–12 minutes until just tender. Drain well, toss the pasta in melted butter and finely grated Parmesan cheese and serve at once.

Gnocchi di patate

Serves 4

Light gnocchi made with potatoes and served, simply, with grated Parmesan cheese.

50 g (2 oz) Parmesan cheese
675 g (1½ lb) cooked potatoes
125 g (5 oz) plain flour

1 large egg
¾ teaspoon baking powder
salt
50 g (2 oz) butter

USE THE GRATING DISC Grate the Parmesan cheese through the grating disc and remove the cheese from the bowl.

USE THE METAL BLADE Combine the potatoes with the flour, egg and baking powder in the Magimix bowl and season with salt. Process until the mixture forms a smooth dough.

Turn onto a floured board and roll into a long thin sausage about the thickness of a finger. Cut into 2.5 cm (1 in.) long pieces pinching the ends of the pieces lightly between the thumb and finger to seal and flatten them.

Drop the gnocchi, a few at a time, into a large pan of salted water and cook for 3 minutes until the gnocchi rise to the surface. Remove them with a slotted spoon draining them well, place each batch in a well buttered baking dish and keep warm while making the rest.

Dot the gnocchi with butter and sprinkle them with Parmesan cheese before serving.

Cannelloni with chicken and spinach

Serves 4

450 g (1 lb) fresh spinach
1 onion
225 g (8 oz) cooked chicken
8 prepared cannelloni tubes
1 tablespoon olive or vegetable oil
50 g (2 oz) Parmesan cheese

100 g (4 oz) Cheddar cheese
50 g (2 oz) butter
salt and freshly ground black pepper
25 g (1 oz) flour
3 dl (½ pint) milk

Wash the spinach and cook it in a little boiling salted water until just tender. Drain well, place the spinach in a colander and press out all the cooking water. Peel and roughly chop the onion. Roughly chop the chicken.

Cook the cannelloni in boiling salted water with 1 tablespoon oil until tender, drain well, separate and leave to cool.

USE THE
GRATING DISC

Grate the Parmesan cheese through the grating disc and remove the cheese. Grate the Cheddar cheese through the grating disc and remove the cheese.

USE THE
METAL BLADE

Place the chicken in the Magimix bowl and process until the chicken is finely chopped. Remove the chicken.

Place the onion in the Magimix bowl and process until the onion is finely chopped and remove the onion.

Place the spinach in the Magimix bowl and process until the spinach is finely chopped.

Melt 25 g (1 oz) butter in a saucepan. Add the onion and cook over a low heat until the onion is soft and transparent.

Add the spinach and continue to cook over a low heat for 3 minutes. Add the chicken, season with salt and pepper, mix well and remove from the heat. Using a large piping bag, stuff the chicken and spinach mixture into the canelloni tubes and arrange them in a well greased baking dish.

Melt the remaining 25 g (1 oz) butter in a small saucepan. Add the flour and mix well. Gradually blend in the milk, stirring continually over a medium high heat until the sauce comes to the boil and is thick and smooth. Add the Cheddar cheese, season with salt and pepper and simmer, stirring, for 3 minutes. Pour the sauce over the stuffed cannelloni, sprinkle over the Parmesan and bake in a moderate oven (180°C, 350°F, Reg. 4) for 20–25 minutes until the dish is hot through and the top is bubbling and lightly golden brown.

Vegetable dishes

Potatoes with leeks and onions

Serves 4

675 g (1½ lb) potatoes
1 leek
2 onions
50 g (2 oz) butter

salt and freshly ground
black pepper
3 dl (½ pint) milk
breadcrumbs
50 g (2 oz) melted butter

USE THE
SLICING DISC

Cut most of the green part off the leek and wash the white part thoroughly. Slice the onions and leek through the slicing disc. Remove the onion and leek from the Magimix bowl. Peel the potatoes and if they are small leave whole. If they are large cut them in half lengthwise. Slice potatoes through the slicing disc.

Melt 50 g (2 oz) butter in a large saucepan and fry all the vegetables together for 5 minutes turning them over carefully to prevent sticking. Butter a fireproof dish well and transfer the vegetables to the dish. Season well with salt and freshly ground black pepper and pour over the milk. Sprinkle the surface with enough breadcrumbs to form a good layer and dribble over the melted butter.

Bake in a very moderate oven (170°C, 325°F, Reg. 3) for 1½ hours until the potatoes are soft and the top is brown and bubbling.

119

Pommes de terre Grenoble

Serves 4

675 g (1½ lb) potatoes
salt and freshly ground
  black pepper

2 cloves garlic, crushed
3 dl (½ pint) milk
25 g (1 oz) butter

USE THE
SLICING DISC

Peel the potatoes and cut them in half lengthwise if they are too large to fit into the feed tube. Slice the potatoes through the slicing disc.

Well butter a fireproof dish. Line the bottom of the dish with a layer of overlapping slices of potato and season with salt, freshly ground black pepper and a little of the crushed garlic. Continue the layers, seasoning each one, until all the potatoes are used up.

Pour the milk over the potatoes and dot with the butter cut into pea sized pieces. Cook in a moderate oven (180°C, 350°F, Reg. 4) for 1½ hours.

Pommes de terre boulangère

Serves 4

675 g (1½ lb) potatoes
2 onions
25 g (1 oz) butter

salt and freshly ground
  black pepper
3 dl (½ pint) stock

Peel the potatoes and cut them in half lengthwise. Peel and halve the onions. Butter a fireproof dish.

USE THE
SLICING DISC

Slice the onions through the slicing disc. Remove the onions.

Melt the butter in a frying pan and add the onions. Cook the onions over a low heat until soft and transparent. Arrange half the onions in the bottom of the fireproof dish.

Slice the potatoes through the slicing disc. Arrange half the potato slices in an overlapping layer on top of the onions. Season well with salt and freshly ground black pepper. Arrange the remaining onions on top of the potatoes and then the rest of the potatoes on top. Season again with salt and pepper.

Pour over the stock and bake in a moderate oven (180°C, 350°F, Reg. 4) for 1½ hours.

Pommes Dorian

Serves 4–5

675 g (1½ lb) potatoes	50 g (2 oz) butter
2 leeks	3 dl (½ pint) milk
37 g (1½ oz) Cheddar	salt and freshly ground
cheese	black pepper

Peel the potatoes. Wash and trim the leeks.

USE THE
GRATING DISC Grate the cheese through the grating disc. Remove the
Cheese.

USE THE
SLICING DISC Slice the leeks through the slicing disc. Remove the
leeks.

USE THE
CHIPPING DISC Chip the potatoes through the chipping disc.

Lightly butter a baking dish. Mix the chipped potatoes and leeks together in the dish and spread over the grated cheese. Pour over the milk, dot with the remaining butter, season with salt and pepper, cover tightly with foil and bake in a moderate oven (180°C, 350°F, Reg. 4) for 1 hour. Remove the foil and cook for a further 15 minutes or until the potatoes are tender and the top is a nice golden brown.

Purée of lentils

Serves 4–6

A good dish to serve with a rich main course such as hare, venison or baked gammon.

450 g (1 lb) lentils	50 g (2 oz) butter
1 onion	1.2 dl (4 fl. oz) single
1 carrot	cream
salt	freshly ground black pepper
2 bay leaves	

Cover the lentils with cold water and leave them to soak overnight.

Peel and roughly chop the onion and carrot.

Place the soaked lentils with their liquid in a pan with the onion, carrot, salt and bay leaves. Add enough water to come about 1 cm (½ in.) above the ingredients and bring them to the boil. Cover and simmer over a low heat for about 1½ hours until the lentils are quite soft. Drain well and remove the bay leaves.

Put the lentils, onion and carrot in the Magimix bowl and process until they are reduced to a smooth purée.

Turn the purée into a clean pan and heat through. Beat in the butter and cream and season with salt and freshly ground black pepper.

Purée freneuse

An unusual and delectable purée of turnips with rice, herbs and garlic. A dish to surprise your guests and add interest to almost any main course.

Serves 6

3 cloves garlic
350 g (12 oz) white turnips
1 small bunch parsley
225 g (8 oz) rice
6 dl (1 pint) milk
25 g (1 oz) butter

¼ teaspoon dried thyme
1 bay leaf
salt
freshly ground black pepper
pinch nutmeg
2 tablespoons double cream

Crush the garlic with the back of a fork. Peel and roughly chop the turnips. Remove the tough stalks from the parsley.

Combine the rice, milk, butter, garlic, thyme and bay leaf in a saucepan. Season with salt, bring to the boil and cook over a low heat, stirring occasionally, for 10 minutes. Add the turnips, bring back to the boil and simmer for a further 15 minutes, stirring every now and then to prevent sticking, until the turnips are tender and the liquid is absorbed into the ingredients. Remove the bay leaf.

Place the parsley leaves in the Magimix bowl and process until the leaves are finely chopped. Remove the parsley.

Place the rice and turnips in the Magimix bowl and process until the ingredients are reduced to a smooth puree. Season with salt, pepper and a little ground nutmeg and add the cream. Process until the ingredients are well mixed.

Return the purée to a clean pan, heat through and pile onto a serving dish. Sprinkle over the chopped parsley before serving.

122

Purée of parsnip and celery

Serves 4

An unusual and very delicious dish that goes well with almost any main course and can take the place of potatoes. Add some chopped ham to the purée to turn this into an inexpensive main course.

1 parsnip
1 head celery
salt
100 g (4 oz) Cheddar cheese

2 slices white bread
1.5 dl ($\frac{1}{4}$ pint) milk
2 eggs
pepper and a pinch nutmeg

Peel and roughly chop the parsnip. Remove the tops and leaves of the celery and roughly chop the stalks. Place the parsnip and celery in a saucepan, cover with cold water, season with a little salt, bring to the boil and simmer until the vegetables are tender. Drain well.

USE THE
GRATING DISC

Grate the cheese through the grating disc and remove from the bowl.

USE THE
METAL BLADE

Remove the crusts from the bread, break up the slices, place them in the Magimix bowl and process until reduced to coarse breadcrumbs. Remove the breadcrumbs.

Place the vegetables in the Magimix bowl and process until puréed. Add the milk, eggs and three-quarters of the cheese. Season with salt, pepper and a pinch of nutmeg and process until smooth. Pile purée into lightly greased baking dish, top with the remainder of the cheese and the breadcrumbs mixed together and bake in a moderate oven (180°C, 350°F, Reg. 4) for 15 minutes until golden brown.

Puréed cauliflower

Serves 4

When cauliflowers are slightly on the large side and a bit past their prime this makes a delicious dish to serve with chicken or fish dishes.

1 cauliflower
75 g (3 oz) butter

salt and freshly ground black pepper

Steam the cauliflower until tender.

USE THE
METAL BLADE

Place the cauliflower in the Magimix bowl with 50g (2 oz) of the butter and process until smooth. Season with

123

salt and freshly ground black pepper and switch the machine on and off to mix in the seasonings.

Transfer to a heated serving dish and dot with the remaining butter.

Note Puréed cauliflower is also delicious fried into a crisp cake. Heat 4 tablespoons vegetable oil in a non-stick pan. Add 1 large finely chopped clove garlic and cook over a low heat until the garlic is transparent. Add the cauliflower and press down firmly into the pan. Cook over a moderate heat until the bottom is crisply golden brown. Dot with butter and brown the top of the cauliflower purée under a hot grill. Invert onto a warmed dish to serve.

Purée of asparagus

Serves 4

It seems almost sacrilege to purée asparagus but if you grow your own you may sometimes end up with those rather weedy stalks, or you may be able to buy inexpensive, inferior stalks at the height of the season; when that is the case do try this really delicious purée which will grace almost any main course.

675 g (1½ lb) asparagus
37 g (1¼ oz) stale white bread with the crusts removed
25 g (1 oz) Parmesan cheese
salt

75 g (3 oz) butter
scant tablespoon flour
1.8 dl (6 fl. oz) double cream
freshly ground black pepper
pinch ground nutmeg

Cut off any hard, white and corey stems of the asparagus. Cut off and reserve the heads and roughly chop the stalks. Break up the bread and Parmesan cheese.

Bring a large pan of salt water to the boil. Plunge in the stalks and cook for 10 minutes. Add the asparagus heads and continue to cook for a further 5 minutes or until the stalks and heads are tender. Drain, and rinse in cold water. Drain well.

USE THE
METAL BLADE

Put the Parmesan in the Magimix bowl and process until the Parmesan is finely ground. Add the bread to the Parmesan and process until the bread is reduced to fairly fine breadcrumbs. Remove the bread and Parmesan.

Place the asparagus stalks and tips in the Magimix bowl and process until the asparagus is reduced to a purée.

124

Melt 50 g (2 oz) butter in a saucepan, add the asparagus and mix well. Sprinkle over the flour, mix well and cook over a low heat, stirring, for 2 minutes. Gradually blend in the cream and heat through. Season with salt, freshly ground black pepper and nutmeg, mix well and turn onto a lightly greased fireproof serving dish. Sprinkle over the breadcrumbs and cheese and dot with the remaining butter. Put the dish under a hot grill and cook for 3–4 minutes until the top is golden brown and bubbling.

Purée of celery root and potatoes

Serves 4–6

450 g (1lb) celeriac
1 teaspoon lemon juice
salt and freshly ground
*   black pepper*

450 g (1 lb) potatoes
62 g (2½ oz) butter

Peel and roughly chop the celeriac, cover it in a pan with cold water and add the lemon juice and a little salt. Bring to the boil and cook for about 30 minutes until tender.

Peel and roughly chop the potatoes and cover with cold water. Season with salt, bring to the boil and cook for about 30 minutes until tender.

Drain the vegetables well.

USE THE
METAL BLADE

Place the celeriac and potatoes in the Magimix bowl (you may have to do this in two steps) and add 50 g (2 oz butter. Process until reduced to a smooth purée. Season with salt and freshly ground black pepper and switch the machine on and off to mix.

Pile the purée onto a heated serving dish and dot with the remaining butter.

Scalloped potatoes and celeriac

Serves 6

A delicious combination cooked in a mixture of stock and cream and topped with golden brown Gruyère cheese.

50 g (2 oz) Gruyère cheese
450 g (1 lb) celeriac
1 teaspoon lemon juice
450 g (1 lb) potatoes
50 g (2 oz) butter cut into
*   small pieces*

salt and freshly ground
*   black pepper*
3 dl (½ pint) chicken stock
1.5 dl (¼pint) double cream

USE THE
GRATING DISC

Grate the cheese through the grating disc and set to one side.

125

Peel the celeriac, and slice through the slicing disc. Cover at once with cold water mixed with the lemon juice. Peel the potatoes and slice them through the slicing disc.

Drain the celeriac. Place a layer of potatoes in a buttered baking dish, cover with a layer of celeriac, dot with a little butter and season with salt and freshly ground black pepper. Fill the dish with alternate layers of celeriac and potatoes finishing with potatoes. Mix the stock and cream and pour over the vegetables. Dot with butter, cover with foil and bake in a moderate oven (180°C, 350°F, Reg. 4) for 50 minutes until vegetables are soft. Remove the foil, sprinkle over the cheese and return to the oven for 10 minutes until cheese has melted and is golden brown.

Purée of courgettes with herbs

Serves 6

4 sprigs chervil
1 small sprig savory
675 g (1½ lb) courgettes
37 g (1½ oz) butter

salt and freshly ground
black pepper
2 tablespoons double cream

Remove the stalks from the chervil and the savory.

Place the herbs in the Magimix bowl and process until the herbs are finely chopped. Remove the herbs.

Slice the courgettes through the slicing disc.

Melt the butter in a large saucepan. Add the courgettes, season with salt and freshly ground black pepper, cover and simmer over a low heat, stirring to prevent sticking, until the courgettes are soft.

Transfer the courgettes to the Magimix bowl and process until reduced to a purée. Add the herbs and cream, check seasoning and process for just a few seconds until the ingredients are mixed.

Pile onto a warm serving dish and heat through before serving.

Parslied courgettes with cheese

Serves 6

4 sprigs parsley
37 g (1½ oz) Parmesan
   cheese
675 g (1½ lb) small
   courgettes

37 g (1½ oz) butter
salt and freshly ground
   black pepper

Remove the parsley stalks. Break the Parmesan into small pieces. Wash and dry the courgettes if necessary.

USE THE
METAL BLADE

Put the Parmesan cheese into the Magimix bowl and process until the cheese is reduced to a coarse powder. Remove the cheese. Place the parsley leaves in the Magimix bowl and process until the leaves are finely chopped. Remove the parsley.

USE THE
SLICING DISC

Slice the courgettes through the slicing disc.
   Melt the butter in a large heavy frying pan. Add the courgettes and cook over a medium high heat for 3 minutes. Turn over the slices, sprinkle over the parsley, season with salt and freshly ground black pepper and sprinkle over the cheese.
   Cook for just long enough to melt the cheese and cook the slices. Serve at once.

Purée of courgettes

Serves 6

If you grow your own vegetables you may well find you have a glut of courgettes if the weather is hot. This makes an unusual and delicious way of serving them.

450 g (1 lb) courgettes
3 slices white bread
3 eggs

salt and freshly ground
   black pepper

Peel the courgettes and cook them in boiling, salted water for about 5 minutes until just soft. Drain off the cooking liquid. Remove the crusts from the bread and soak the slices in the courgette cooking liquid until soft. Drain off excess liquid.

USE THE
METAL BLADE

Combine the courgettes, bread and eggs in the Magimix bowl, season with salt and pepper and process until the mixture is smooth.

127

Butter a soufflé dish, pour in the courgette mixture and bake in a preheated moderate oven (180°C, 350°F, Reg. 4) for 35 minutes.

Serve at once.

Sliced courgettes and mushrooms

Serves 4

3 sprigs parsley
450 g (1 lb) courgettes
100 g (4 oz) firm button mushrooms

37 g (1½ oz) butter
salt and freshly ground black pepper
juice of ½ a lemon

Remove the stalks from the parsley. Wash and dry the courgettes if necessary.

USE THE
METAL BLADE

Place the parsley in the Magimix bowl and process until finely chopped. Remove the parsley.

USE THE
SLICING DISC

Slice the courgettes and mushrooms through the slicing disc. Melt the butter in a large, heavy frying pan. Add the courgettes and mushrooms, cover and cook over a low heat for about 5 minutes until the ingredients are just tender. Season well with salt and pepper, sprinkle over the lemon juice and parsley and turn onto a serving dish.

Mushroom and potatoes with sour cream

Serves 6

1 small onion
6 medium potatoes
225 g (8 oz) firm button mushrooms

25 g (1 oz) butter
salt and freshly ground black pepper
1 carton (1.5 dl/5 fl. oz) sour cream

USE THE
METAL BLADE

Peel and quarter the onion, put it into the Magimix bowl and process until finely chopped. Remove the onion.

Cook the potatoes in their skins in boiling salted water for 20 minutes. Drain, cool and remove the skins.

USE THE
SLICING DISC

Slice the mushrooms through the slicing disc and remove from the bowl. Slice the potatoes through the slicing disc.

Heat the butter in a frying pan. Add the onion and cook

over a low heat until soft and transparent. Add the sliced mushrooms and cook for 2 minutes over a medium heat.

Well grease a baking dish and fill it with layers of potatoes and mushrooms, seasoning the layers with salt and pepper and finishing with a layer of potatoes. Pour over the sour cream and bake in a moderate oven (180°C, 350°F, Reg. 4) for 30 minutes.

Carrots fried in butter

Serves 4

One of the most delicious ways of cooking carrots.

small bunch parsley
675 g (1¼ lb) carrots
50 g (2 oz) butter

salt and freshly ground
black pepper

USE THE
METAL BLADE

Remove the stalks from the parsley, place the leaves in the Magimix and process until finely chopped. Remove the parsley and set aside.

Peel the carrots.

USE THE
CHIPPING DISC

Process the carrots through the chipping disc.

Cook the carrots in boiling salted water for 6 minutes until three-quarters cooked. Drain well. Heat the butter in a large frying pan. Add the carrots and cook over a medium high heat, shaking the pan to prevent sticking, until the carrots are lightly browned and tender.

Season with salt and freshly ground black pepper and transfer to a heated serving dish. Sprinkle over the parsley before serving.

Aubergine casserole

Serves 4

small bunch parsley
50 g (2 oz) Parmesan
cheese
1 (400 g/14 oz) can
tomatoes
4 small aubergines
4 courgettes

1½ tablespoons vegetable
oil
1 clove garlic
salt and freshly ground
black pepper
pinch of thyme and
oregano

USE THE
METAL BLADE

Remove the parsley stalks (these can be used in the stock pot) and put the leaves in the Magimix bowl. Process until the parsley is finely chopped and set on one side.

129

Break up the Parmesan cheese, put it into the Magimix bowl and process until the cheese is powdered. Remove the cheese and set on one side.

Put the tomatoes in the Magimix bowl and process until they are roughly chopped. Remove tomatoes and set on one side.

USE THE
SLICING DISC
Thinly peel the aubergines and slice them with the slicing disc. Slice the courgettes without peeling. Remove the aubergines and courgettes from the Magimix bowl and place them in an oiled casserole. Peel and finely chop the garlic and add it to the vegetables. Season the tomatoes with salt and black pepper and mix in the tyme and oregano. Pour the tomatoes over the vegetables and top with the grated Parmesan cheese. Bake in a hot oven (200°C, 400°F, Reg. 6) for about 20 minutes until the vegetables are soft and the topping is golden brown.

Sprinkle with the chopped parsley before serving.

Cabbage with cream and horseradish

Serves 4–6

*1 medium drumhead
    cabbage
1 piece, 2.5 cm (1 in.) long,
    horseradish root*

*3 dl ($\frac{1}{2}$ pint) single cream
salt, freshly ground black
    pepper and a pinch
    nutmeg*

Quarter the cabbage and remove the tough stalk. Peel the horseradish root.

USE THE
GRATING DISC
Grate the horseradish root through the grating disc. Remove the horseradish.

USE THE
SLICING DISC
Slice the cabbage through the slicing disc. Bring a large saucepan of salted water to the boil. Add the cabbage and cook over a high heat for 10 minutes. Drain the cabbage well and return it to the saucepan with the cream and horseradish. Season with salt, pepper and a pinch of nutmeg. Heat through stirring continually over a low heat and cooking until the cabbage is tender.

Beetroot in horseradish and cheese sauce

Serves 4

100 g (4 oz) Cheddar cheese
4 medium cooked beetroot
25 g (1 oz) butter
1½ tablespoons flour

3 dl (½ pint) milk
1 tablespoon made horseradish sauce
salt and freshly ground black pepper

USE THE
GRATING DISC

Grate the cheese through the grating disc and set on one side.

USE THE
SLICING DISC

Slice the beetroot through the slicing disc and set on one side. Melt the butter in a saucepan. Add the flour and mix well. Gradually blend in the milk, stirring continually, over a medium heat until the sauce is thick and smooth. Add the horseradish sauce, half the cheese, season with salt and pepper and continue to cook stirring all the time, over a medium heat until the cheese has melted.

Add the beetroot slices, mix lightly and turn into a fireproof serving dish. Sprinkle over the remaining grated cheese and bake in a moderately hot oven (190°C, 375°F, Reg. 5) for 15 minutes until the top of the dish is bubbling and golden.

Beetroot in a rich cheese sauce

Serves 6

12 small cooked beetroot
25 g (1 oz) Parmesan cheese
6 spring onions
12 g (½ oz) butter

1 tablespoon flour
3 dl (½ pint) single cream
salt and freshly ground black pepper

Peel the beetroot. Break up the Parmesan. Trim and roughly chop the spring onions.

USE THE
METAL BLADE

Place the Parmesan cheese in the Magimix bowl and process until the cheese is reduced to a fine powder. Remove the cheese. Place the spring onions in the Magimix bowl and process until the onions are finely chopped.

USE THE
SLICING DISC

Slice the beetroot through the slicing disc.

Melt the butter in a saucepan. Add the flour and mix well. Gradually blend in the cream, stirring continually over a medium heat without allowing the sauce to boil.

131

Add the spring onions, season with salt and freshly ground black pepper and simmer very slowly for 3 minutes.

Place the beetroot in a shallow fireproof serving dish. Pour over the sauce, sprinkle with the cheese and put under a hot grill until the top is golden brown and the dish is hot through.

Baked fennel with tomatoes

Serves 6

A deliciously rich vegetable dish that I often serve as a first course.

4 fennel bulbs
1 onion
50 g (2 oz) Parmesan
*   cheese*
75 g (3 oz) white bread
*   with the crusts removed*
6 tablespoons olive oil

salt and freshly ground
*   black pepper*
1 clove garlic
grated rind of ½ a lemon
1 medium tin tomatoes
pinch oregano

Remove any tough outer leaves of the fennel and trim off any green leaves from the top of the bulbs. Peel the onion. Break up the Parmesan cheese and bread.

USE THE
SLICING DISC

Slice the onion through the slicing disc. Remove the onion. Slice the fennel through the slicing disc. Remove the fennel and wash the bowl. Heat the oil in a large heavy frying pan Add the onion and cook over a low heat until the onion is soft and transparent. Add the fennel slices and season with salt and pepper. Cook over a medium heat stirring now and then until the fennel has turned a golden colour and is almost tender. This will take about 20 minutes.

USE THE
METAL BLADE

Place the cheese in the Magimix bowl and process until the cheese is reduced to a powder. Add the bread and garlic to the cheese and process until the bread is reduced to coarse breadcrumbs. Add the lemon rind and process for long enough to mix the ingredients. Remove the bread mixture.

Place the tomatoes in the Magimix bowl with the oregano and process for just long enough to break up the tomatoes.

Drain off the oil from the onion and fennel and place the vegetables in a fireproof serving dish. Cover with the tomatoes and top with the breadcrumb and cheese mixture. Dribble over the oil from the pan and bake in a hot oven (200°C, 400°F, Reg. 6) for about 15 minutes until the topping is crisp and golden brown and the dish is hot through.

Ratatouille of fennel

Serves 4

Whether there is any truth in the idea that fennel is an aphrodisiac or not I have never managed to find out but this vegetable is certainly a great asset to winter salads.

In this dish the fennel can either be served hot or cold and it makes a very acceptable first course.

4 sprigs parsley
2 bulbs fennel
450 g (1 lb) ripe tomatoes
2 onions
2 courgettes

3 tablespoons olive oil
salt and freshly ground
*   black pepper*
small sprig thyme
1 bay leaf

USE THE
METAL BLADE

Remove the parsley stalks, place the leaves in the Magimix bowl and process until finely chopped. Remove the parsley.

Remove any discoloured outsides of the fennel and the green tops and cut each bulb in half.

Peel the tomatoes by covering them with boiling water for 1 minute and then draining and sliding off the skins. Quarter the tomatoes and place them in the Magimix bowl. Process until roughly chopped and remove.

USE THE
SLICING DISC

Peel the onions and slice them through the slicing disc. Remove the onions. Slice the courgettes through the slicing disc. Remove the courgettes.

Heat the oil in a heavy based saucepan or fireproof casserole. Add the onion and cook over a low heat until the onion is soft and transparent. Place the fennel, flat side down, on the onion and cover with the tomatoes and then a layer of the courgettes, seasoning the ingredients with salt and freshly ground black pepper. Add the thyme and bay leaf. Cover the pan tightly and cook over a very low heat for 1 hour until the fennel is tender. Uncover the dish, increase the heat and cook until the excess juice has evaporated and the ingredients are moist but not soggy.

Serve hot or chilled, sprinkled with the finely chopped parsley.

Escalloped sweetcorn

Serves 4

100 g (4 oz) cooked
   sweetcorn (or drained
   tinned sweetcorn)
2 eggs
50 g (2 oz) melted butter
   (cooled)

1 teaspoon sugar
$\frac{1}{4}$ teaspoon nutmeg
1.5 dl ($\frac{1}{4}$ pint) milk
salt and freshly ground
   black pepper

USE THE
METAL BLADE

Combine all the ingredients in the Magimix bowl and process until the sweetcorn is finely chopped.

Lightly grease a baking dish with butter, pour in the
sweetcorn mixture and bake in a moderate oven (180°C,
350°F, Reg. 4) for 20 minutes until just set. Serve hot.

Celeriac in mayonnaise

I find this an invaluable topping for lobster or salmon
when you want a small amount of expensive fish to stretch
a long way. This delicious mixture can also be used to top
more mundane, cold, poached fish like cod or halibut.

2 celeriac roots
pinch salt and sugar
1 tablespoon lemon juice
1.5 dl ($\frac{1}{4}$ pint) mayonnaise

1 tablespoon tomato
   ketchup
pepper

USE THE METAL
CHIPPER BLADE

Peel the celeriac, cut them into quarters and cut them
through the chipper blade. Plunge celeriac into boiling
water to which a little salt, sugar and the lemon juice has
been added and blanch for 2 minutes. Drain well and
leave to cool.

Combine the mayonnaise with the tomato ketchup and
season with salt and pepper. Add the cooled celeriac and
toss lightly to mix. Chill before serving.

Salads and slimming dishes

Slimming with the aid of your Magimix food processor

Slimming is never easy and one of the major problems those who try and lose a few pounds come up against is the dreariness that so often goes hand in hand with non-fattening foods. Here, once more, the Magimix food processor comes into its own providing exciting sauces, dressings and marinades which will help to make a calorie-controlled diet something you can actually look forward to.

Use the Magimix slicing and grating discs to make gay and varied salads; use the Magimix metal blade to beat up low calorie sauces and salad dressings and use the fruit and vegetable juice extractor to produce health-giving fresh fruit and vegetable juice.

Forest Mere salad

Serves 4

One of the hazards of being a cookery writer is that of putting on too much weight as you test recipes and find, if you are me, it impossible to resist all the temptations that come your way in the form of delicious, calorie-full food.

135

A week at the health farm Forest Mere put me right and also produced a number of delicious recipes for me to take home that were both healthy and non-fattening.

1 small clove garlic
1 teaspoon sea salt
¼ teaspoon paprika pepper
1 tablespoon olive oil
2 tablespoons lemon juice
1 medium leek

1 small cauliflower
50 g (2 oz) Caerphilly
* cheese*
100 g (4 oz) cashew nuts
50 g (2 oz) sultanas

USE THE
METAL BLADE

Place the garlic, salt, paprika, olive oil and lemon juice in the Magimix bowl and process until the ingredients are well mixed. Remove the dressing.

Cut off the top and outside tough leaves of the leek. Remove the green leaves of the cauliflower.

USE THE
SLICING DISC

Slice the leek.

USE THE
GRATING DISC

Grate the cauliflower, cheese and nuts through the grating disc. Combine all the ingredients, pour over the dressing and toss lightly with two forks to mix. Chill before serving.

Cauliflower salad with cheese

Serves 4

1 small head cauliflower
50 g (2 oz) Cheddar cheese

1.5 dl (¼ pint) mayonnaise
few drops Tabasco sauce

Remove the outside leaves of the cauliflower, trim off the stalk and divide the head into florettes.

USE THE
GRATING DISC

Grate the cheese through the grating disc.

USE THE
METAL BLADE

Add the mayonnaise to the cheese in the Magimix bowl and flavour with a few drops Tabasco sauce. Process for just long enough to blend the ingredients.

Spoon the dressing over the cauliflower florettes and chill before serving.

Cauliflower salad

Serves 4

1 cauliflower
8 black olives
1 green pepper
1 teaspoon Dijon mustard
1.5 dl (¼ pint) olive oil

1 tablespoon white wine
  vinegar
2 tablespoons yoghurt
salt and freshly ground
  black pepper

Remove the outer leaves of the cauliflower, separate the head into florettes and cook them in boiling, salted water until just tender but still crunchy. Drain well and leave to cool.

Remove the stones from the olives. Remove the seeds and core from the pepper and roughly chop the flesh.

USE THE
METAL BLADE

Combine the pepper, olives, mustard, oil, vinegar and yoghurt in the Magimix bowl and season with salt and pepper. Process until the ingredients are well mixed and the pepper and olives are finely chopped.

Pour the dressing over the cauliflower and chill well before serving.

Mushroom and pepper salad

Serves 4–6

100 g (¼ lb) mushrooms
1 small bunch chives or
  spring onion tops
2 green peppers
1 carton yoghurt
  (1.5 dl/5 fl. oz)

1 tablespoon tomato
  ketchup
1 teaspoon lemon juice
salt and paprika pepper

USE THE
SLICING DISC

Slice the mushrooms through the slicing disc and remove the mushrooms. Wipe out the bowl with kitchen paper.

USE THE
METAL BLADE

Place the chives in the Magimix bowl and process until the chives are finely chopped. Remove the core and seeds of the peppers and roughly chop the flesh.

Add the peppers to the chives with the yoghurt, tomato ketchup and lemon juice and season with salt and a little paprika pepper. Process for long enough to finely chop the green peppers.

Pour the dressing over the mushrooms, mix lightly and chill before serving.

Pepper, onion and olive salad

Serves 4

2 red peppers
1 large mild onion
100 g (4 oz) black olives
3 tablespoons olive oil

1 tablespoon white wine
* vinegar*
salt and freshly ground
* black pepper*

Bake the red peppers in a hot oven for 15 minutes. Cool, slide off the skins and cut into halves. Remove the core and seeds and cut the peppers into thin strips.
  Peel the onion and remove the stones from the olives.

USE THE
SLICING DISC

Thinly slice the onion through the slicing disc. Remove the onion and combine it in a serving dish with the red peppers.

USE THE
METAL BLADE

Combine the olive oil and vinegar in the Magimix bowl and season with salt and pepper. Add the olives and process until the ingredients are well mixed and the olives are finely chopped. Pour the dressing over the onion and peppers and chill well before serving.

Cottage cheese and watercress salad

Crisply fried bacon pieces add a nice bite to this salad.

Serves 2

1 bunch watercress
2 small firm tomatoes
1 grapefruit
4 tablespoons olive oil
1½ tablespoons white wine
* vinegar*
2 teaspoons home-made
* tomato purée (see*
* page 162)*

salt and freshly ground
* black pepper*
2 thin rashers streaky
* bacon*
150 g (5 oz) cottage cheese
pinch of cayenne pepper

Remove the stalks from the watercress. Very thinly slice the tomatoes. Peel the grapefruit, divide into segments and remove the white pith and skin from each segment.

USE THE
METAL BLADE

Combine the olive oil, vinegar and tomato purée in the Magimix bowl and season with salt and freshly ground black pepper. Process until the ingredients are well mixed. Add the watercress leaves and grapefruit segments and process until the leaves and grapefruit are coarsely chopped – do not over-process. Remove the watercress and grapefruit.

Remove the rinds from the bacon and roughly chop the rashers. Place the bacon in the Magimix bowl and process until the bacon is finely chopped. Cook the bacon in a frying pan over a medium high heat, without extra fat, until the bacon is crisp. Drain well on kitchen paper.

Arrange the cottage cheese in a mound on a serving dish and surround with the slices of tomato topped with the watercress and grapefruit mixture. Sprinkle the cheese with a little cayenne pepper and top with the crisp bacon pieces.

Serve chilled.

Raw carrot salad

Serves 4

450 g (1 lb) crisp carrots
2 tablespoons olive oil
2 teaspoons white wine
vinegar

3 tablespoons sour cream
salt and freshly ground
black pepper

Peel the carrots.

USE THE
GRATING DISC

Grate the carrots through the grating disc. Remove the carrots.

USE THE
METAL BLADE

Combine the olive oil, vinegar and sour cream in the Magimix bowl and season with salt and freshly ground black pepper. Process until the ingredients are well mixed.

Pour the dressing over the salad, mix well and chill before serving.

Frank's salad

Serves 4

225 g ($\frac{1}{2}$ lb) cooked
beetroot
4 sticks celery
2 firm eating apples
1 small onion
1 dill pickled cucumber

3 tablespoons olive oil
2 tablespoons white wine
vinegar
2 tablespoons sour cream
salt and freshly ground
black pepper

Roughly chop the beetroot. Trim the celery. Peel and core the apples. Peel and roughly chop the onion. Roughly chop the cucumber.

USE THE
SLICING DISC Slice the celery through the slicing disc. Remove the celery.

USE THE
METAL BLADE Place the apples in the Magimix bowl and process until fairly finely chopped. Remove the apples. Place the beetroot in the Magimix bowl and process until the beetroot is roughly chopped. Add the beetroot to the celery and apple.

Place the onion and cucumber in the Magimix bowl and process until the onion and cucumber are coarsely chopped. Add the olive oil, vinegar and sour cream, season with salt and pepper and process for just long enough to incorporate the ingredients.

Add the dressing to the beetroot, celery and apple, mix lightly and chill before serving.

Russian chicken salad

Serves 4–6

2 firm eating apples	*1 teaspoon lemon juice*
½ small cabbage	*1.5 dl (¼ pint) mayonnaise*
350–450 g (12–16 oz)	*(see page 147)*
cooked chicken	*1 tablespoon pickled*
1 dill pickled cucumber	*cucumber liquid*
225 g (8 oz) cooked French	*salt*
beans	*1 teaspoon paprika pepper*

Peel and core the apples. Remove the hard core of the cabbage. Roughly chop the chicken. Roughly chop the cucumber. Slice the beans.

USE THE
SLICING DISC Shred the cabbage through the slicing disc and remove the cabbage. Slice the apples through the slicing disc, sprinkle over the lemon juice and leave them on one side.

USE THE
METAL BLADE Place the chicken and cucumber in the Magimix bowl with the mayonnaise and pickled cucumber liquid. Season with salt and paprika pepper and process for just long enough for the chicken and cucumber to be roughly chopped. Add the apples and beans to the chicken mayonnaise in the Magimix bowl and switch on and off to incorporate the ingredients.

Arrange the shredded cabbage around a serving dish and pile the chicken salad in the centre.

Grilled spring chicken with a watercress salad

Serves 4

150 g (2 oz) Gruyère cheese
12 g (½ oz) butter
2 spring chickens, halved
juice of 2 lemons
salt and freshly ground black pepper
2 bunches watercress
1 carton yoghurt (1.5 dl/5 fl. oz)

USE THE GRATING DISC

Grate the cheese through the grating disc.

Melt the butter. Brush the chicken halves on both sides with the juice of 1 lemon, season with salt and freshly ground black pepper and then brush with the melted butter. Grill under a medium heat, basting frequently with the juices in the pan for 5 minutes. Turn over and grill for a further 5 minutes. Cover the breast sides of the chicken with grated cheese, return under the grill and cook for a further 10 minutes.

Remove the coarse stems of the watercress.

USE THE METAL BLADE

Place the yoghurt, watercress leaves and the juice of 1 lemon in the Magimix bowl and season with salt and freshly ground black pepper. Process until the leaves are roughly chopped and turn into a serving bowl.

Serve the hot chicken with the watercress salad.

Grilled chicken

Serves 6

2 onions
5 cloves garlic
a piece of fresh ginger root 2.5 cm (1 in.) long
2 green chillis
½ teaspoon ground cumin
1 tablespoon ground coriander
1.5 dl (¼ pint) white wine or cider vinegar
salt and freshly ground black pepper
1.5 dl (¼ pint) olive oil or vegetable oil
6 chicken joints

Peel and quarter the onions. Peel the garlic. Peel and roughly chop the ginger. Remove the stalks and roughly chop the chillis.

USE THE METAL BLADE

Place the onions, garlic, ginger, chillis, cumin, coriander and vinegar in the Magimix bowl, season with salt and freshly ground black pepper and process until the mixture is reduced to a purée. With the motor running, pour the oil through the feed tube and process until the ingredients are well mixed.

Lightly score the chicken joints at 1 cm ($\frac{1}{2}$ in.) intervals. Place them in a bowl, pour over the marinade and leave to stand in a cool place for at least 8 hours turning the joints now and then to ensure they are well soaked.

Grill the chicken joints under a medium high heat, turning them to ensure even cooking and basting them with some of the marinade for about 30 minutes or until golden brown and well cooked throughout.

Ham and fennel salad

1 tablespoon parsley or basil leaves
100 g (4 oz) ham
4 fennel roots

vinaigrette dressing (see page 152)
6 hard-boiled eggs
1.5 dl ($\frac{1}{4}$ pint) mayonnaise (see page 147)

USE THE
METAL BLADE

Place the parsley or basil leaves in the Magimix bowl and process until finely chopped. Remove the herbs. Roughly chop the ham, place it in the Magimix bowl and process until chopped to the size of peas. Remove the ham.

USE THE
SLICING DISC

Trim off any discoloured leaves and the green tops of the fennel roots, cut each in half and slice through the slicing blade. Place the fennel in a bowl, add the ham, pour over the vinaigrette sauce, mix well and chill for 30 minutes.

USE THE
METAL BLADE

Halve the hard-boiled eggs and place the yolks in the Magimix bowl with the mayonnaise. Process until smooth. Fill the egg whites with the mixture.

Arrange the fennel and ham in the centre of a serving dish and surround with the stuffed hard-boiled eggs.

Courgettes and bacon salad

Serves 4

450 g (1lb) small courgettes
4 thin rashers streaky bacon
small bunch chives or spring onion tops
4 leaves fresh tarragon

3 tablespoons olive oil
$\frac{1}{2}$ teaspoon Dijon mustard
1 tablespoon white wine wine vinegar
salt and freshly ground black pepper

Remove the rind from the bacon and roughly chop it.

142

Slice the courgettes through the slicing disc and arrange them in a shallow serving dish.

Fry the bacon until crisp without using any extra fat. Drain the bacon on kitchen paper and leave to cool.

Place the chives and tarragon in the Magimix bowl and process until the herbs and finely chopped. Add the bacon and continue to process until the bacon is fairly finely shopped. Add the olive oil, mustard and vinegar, season with salt and pepper and process until the ingredients are well mixed.

Pour the dressing over the courgettes and chill the salad before serving.

Mushroom and sour cream salad

Serves 4

100 g (4 oz) firm button mushrooms
2 spring onions
1 teaspoon lemon juice

1 carton sour cream (1.5 dl/5 fl. oz)
salt and freshly ground black pepper
pinch paprika

Slice the mushrooms and spring onions through the slicing disc and sprinkle the sliced ingredients with the lemon juice.

Season the sour cream with salt, pepper and a pinch of paprika and lightly fold in the mushrooms and spring onions.

Chill before serving.

Slimmer's dip

1 spring onion
225 g ($\frac{1}{2}$ lb) cottage cheese

4 tablespoons yoghurt
$\frac{1}{4}$ teaspoon paprika pepper

Roughly chop the spring onion and put it in the Magimix bowl. Process until the spring onion is reduced to a pulp. (You may have to stop the machine and scrape down the sides with a plastic spatula once or twice during processing). Add the remaining ingredients and process until smooth.

Forest Mere yoghurt dressing

A good dressing for all those who should keep away from vegetable oils.

1 teaspoon sea salt
¼ teaspoon paprika pepper
¼ teaspoon dry mustard
4 tablespoons skim milk
  (this can now be bought
  from good dairies)

2 tablespoons white wine
  vinegar
1 egg yolk
2 drops Tabasco sauce
1.5 dl (¼ pint) yoghurt

USE THE
PLASTIC BLADE

Combine all the ingredients except the yoghurt in the Magimix bowl and process until well mixed. Turn the mixture into the top of a double boiler and cook over hot water, stirring constantly, until the mixture thickens and will coat the back of a wooden spoon. Turn into a bowl and leave to get cold.

Mix in the yoghurt and serve chilled.

Low calorie thousand island dressing

This delicious but non-fattening dressing will keep in a screw-top jar for a week.

1 small bunch parsley
1 dill pickled cucumber
1 stick celery
1 clove garlic
2.7 dl (9 fl. oz) tarragon
  vinegar

1 tablespoon
  Worcestershire sauce
1 teaspoon paprika pepper
1 teaspoon Dijon mustard
3 dl (½ pint) tomato juice

Remove the stalks from the parsley. Roughly chop the cucumber and celery. Peel the garlic clove.

USE THE
METAL BLADE

Place the parsley and garlic in the Magimix bowl and process until the parsley leaves are finely chopped. Add the celery and cucumber and continue to process until the ingredients are finely chopped. Add the vinegar, Worcestershire sauce, paprika, Dijon mustard and tomato juice and switch on and off to mix the ingredients.

144

Chinese dressing

A low calorie dressing that is ideal for slimmers.

0.6 g ($\frac{1}{4}$ oz) piece of fresh
  ginger
3 tablespoons lemon juice

3 tablespoons soy sauce
1 tablespoon castor sugar

USE THE
METAL BLADE

Peel the ginger. Place the ginger in the Magimix bowl and process until the ginger is finely chopped. Add the other ingredients and process until well mixed.

Pickle and yoghurt dressing

A sharp, spikey dressing that adds flavour to green or mixed salads.

2 tablespoons mixed
  pickled vegetables
1 carton yoghurt (1.5 dl/
  5 fl. oz)

1 teaspoon Dijon mustard
salt and freshly ground
  black pepper

USE THE
METAL BLADE

Combine the ingredients in the Magimix bowl and season with salt and freshly ground black pepper. Process until the vegetables are finely chopped.

Yoghurt and mushroom sauce

1 bunch parsley
100 g (4 oz) firm button
  mushrooms
butter

1 carton yoghurt (1.5 dl/
  5 fl. oz)
salt and white pepper

Remove the stalks from the parsley.

USE THE
METAL BLADE

Place the parsley leaves in the Magimix bowl and process until the parsley is finely chopped.

USE THE
SLICING DISC

Slice the mushrooms. Melt the butter in a saucepan. Add the parsley and mushrooms and cook over a low heat, stirring lightly now and then, for 4 minutes. Add the yoghurt and mix well. Season with salt and pepper and heat through, stirring – but do not allow to boil.

Serve the sauce with boiled chicken, fish or vegetables.

145

Sauces, dips and sandwich fillings

Making sauces in your Magimix food processor

Sauces can make or mar a dish and, especially where more inexpensive ingredients are concerned, a good sauce can be essential. 'A good cook is known by his sauces' is a popular saying but perfectly competent cooks fall down on their sauce making merely because they may not have the time to perform the elaborate preparations many classic sauces require. With a Magimix food processor all that is changed. Exciting and traditional sauces, even those of the more sophisticated *haute cuisine*, come within the scope of any cook. Chopping, puréeing and blending is done for you, the flavours and aromas of herbs and spices are richly expanded, egg yolks can be beaten into hot liquid without fear of curdling and even tricky mayonnaise or hollandaise can become so simple that they could not even deter the total novice in the kitchen.

Forget forever the sad disappointments of lumpy or curdled creations, forget those dreary bottled parodies of old fashioned sauce and make, in minutes, your own horseradish cream, apple or mint sauce, the all important duxelles and espagnole that helps to give so many dishes a lift, and discover a whole new world of complementary and exotic combinations.

146

Follow your favourite sauce recipes remembering that when a sauce calls for:

long beating – do it in the Magimix food processor
chopped ingredients or herbs – chop them in the Magimix food processor
sliced or grated ingredients – process them in the Magimix food processor
incorporating egg yolks – beat them in smoothly with the Magimix metal blade
puréeing – purée the ingredients in the Magimix food processor.

Magimix mayonnaise

There is all the difference in the world between a really good, classic, mayonnaise and one that does not quite come off. With the Magimix food processor you can be assured of success and of producing a gloriously pale golden sauce that is thick enough to stand a spoon up in and which has the shine of a rich satin.

Do not add the seasoning until the mayonnaise is made and add your oil through the feed tube, with the motor running, in a slow steady stream. Adding a little vinegar to the egg yolks will ensure that your mayonnaise is really thick and will help to prevent curdling.

All the ingredients for a mayonnaise, or any mayonnaise based sauce, should be at the same temperature (i.e. do not attempt to take egg yolks from the refrigerator and combine them with olive oil that has been standing at room temperature).

Pure olive oil is the best oil to use for a mayonnaise but if you have to use a substitute do use a good sunflower oil rather than corn oil which has a slightly strong flavouring.

2 egg yolks
½ teaspoon Dijon mustard
* or dry mustard*

2 tablespoons white wine
* vinegar*
3 dl (½ pint) olive oil
salt and white pepper

USE THE
METAL BLADE

Place the egg yolks and mustard in the Magimix bowl with 1 teaspoon vinegar and process until the egg yolks are well mixed. With the machine switched on, gradually add the olive oil, pouring it in a very slow, steady stream through the feed tube and continue to process until the oil has been used up and the mayonnaise is very thick and shining. Gradually add the remaining vinegar, still with the machine switched on. Stop the machine, season with salt and pepper and process for just long enough to mix in the seasoning.

Spiked mayonnaise

A mayonnaise with a zip to it. Serve it with fish or cold meat or use it as a base for a fish or chicken salad. Use it also as a dressing for potato salad.

1 small bunch parsley
1 small bunch chives
1 clove garlic
1 anchovy fillet

1 teaspoon Dijon mustard
1 hard-boiled egg
4.5 dl ($\frac{3}{4}$ pint) home-made
mayonnaise

USE THE
METAL BLADE

Place the herbs in the Magimix bowl and process until finely chopped. Remove the herbs.
  Place the garlic and anchovy fillet in the Magimix bowl with the mustard and process until the ingredients are smooth. Quarter the hard-boiled egg and add it to the ingredients in the bowl with the mayonnaise and herbs. Process for just long enough to blend the ingredients and finely chop the egg.

Herb mayonnaise

A delicious accompaniment to fish in the place of a tartare sauce.

1 bunch parsley
1 sprig fresh basil
1 egg
1 teaspoon dry mustard
1 tablespoon white wine
* vinegar*

$\frac{1}{2}$ teaspoon lemon juice
salt and freshly ground
* black pepper*
3 dl ($\frac{1}{2}$ pint) olive oil

USE THE
METAL BLADE

Remove the stalks from the parsley and basil. Place the herbs in the Magimix bowl and process until the herbs are finely chopped. Remove the herbs.
  Place the egg in the Magimix bowl with the mustard, vinegar, lemon juice and a little salt and freshly ground black pepper. Process until the ingredients are well blended. With the machine running, gradually add the

olive oil in a steady stream until the mixture begins to thicken and all the oil is used up. Add the herbs and process for a further 10 seconds to blend.

Check the seasoning and add a little more salt and freshly ground black pepper if necessary.

Chilli mayonnaise

You have heard of Jack the Fat and Jean the Lean? Well, Robin and I are like that only in our case the opposites apply to hot and mild. I love anything with chillis, Tabasco sauce or cayenne pepper; Robin likes things smooth and mild. The crunch really comes in sauces when he turns his nose up at anything faintly 'hot', so I have developed a system to get the best of both possible worlds. . . . he has his sauce and I have mine.

This is *my* sauce to serve with hard-boiled eggs, summer salads or fish salads in the place of a plain mayonnaise; I love it, he turns his nose right up at it! It also makes a good barbecue sauce.

1 small red pepper
1.5 dl ($\frac{1}{4}$ pint) home-made or bought mayonnaise
4 tablespoons yoghurt
generous pinch cayenne pepper

2 drops of Tabasco sauce
1 tablespoon tomato ketchup
salt and freshly ground black pepper

Quarter the red pepper and remove the core, white membrane and any seeds.

USE THE METAL BLADE Put the pepper in the Magimix bowl and process until the pepper is finely chopped. Add the remaining ingredients, season with salt and freshly ground black pepper and process until the ingredients are mixed and the pepper is very finely chopped.

Mayonnaise Chantilly

Make the mayonnaise with lemon juice rather than vinegar. Add 4 tablespoons double cream to the finished mayonnaise and process for just long enough to mix the ingredients.

149

Mayonnaise Colée

The mayonnaise that is used to coat cold foods such as chicken joints, salmon or eggs. Gelatine prevents the mayonnaise sliding off the cold ingredients.

Dissolve 0.6 g ($\frac{1}{4}$ oz) gelatine in 2 tablespoons boiling water and add it to the mayonnaise after the sauce has been finished.
   Process for just long enough to mix the ingredients and coat the cooked chicken, fish or eggs with the mayonnaise before it has had time to set.

Mayonnaise escoffier

Finely chop the leaves of 2 sprigs parsley and 2 sprigs chervil with the metal blade before making the mayonnaise. Remove and reserve the herbs. Grate 1 cm ($\frac{1}{2}$ in.) raw horseradish root through the shredding disc and reserve. Add the herbs and horseradish to the finished mayonnaise and process for just long enough to mix the ingredients.

Sauce nicoise

Add 4 tablespoons home-made tomato purée (see page 162) to the finished mayonnaise with 1 crushed garlic clove, 2.5 ml ($\frac{1}{2}$ teaspoon) finely chopped tarragon and a little paprika pepper. Process for long enough to finely chop the garlic and incorporate the ingredients.

Mustard mayonnaise with dill

This is a delicious sauce to serve with fish or eggs in the summer. Leave out the dill and you have a really excellent accompaniment to steak tartare or to very thin slices of underdone roast beef.

Finely chop $\frac{1}{2}$ tablespoon dill leaves with the metal blade and remove them before making the mayonnaise. Add 1 tablespoon of Dijon mustard to the egg yolks before adding the olive oil to the mayonnaise.

Sauce rémoulade

Delicious with eggs and cold cooked vegetables.

Before making the mayonnaise, finely chop the leaves from 2 sprigs of parsley and chervil in the Magimix bowl using the metal blade. When the herbs are finely chopped add 1 teaspoon of capers and 2 cocktail gherkins and process again until the gherkins and capers are finely chopped. Remove and reserve the chopped ingredients before making the mayonnaise.

Add the chopped ingredients to the finished mayonnaise with $\frac{1}{2}$ teaspoon anchovy essence and process for just long enough to mix the ingredients.

Curried mayonnaise

Combine 2 tablespoons home-made tomato purée with 1 teaspoon curry powder and 1 teaspoon lemon juice and cook over a low heat until the curry powder is dissolved. Leave to cool.

Add the curry mixture to the finished mayonnaise with 2 tablespoons of double cream and process until the ingredients are well mixed.

Andalusian sauce

An attractive red sauce to serve with cold fish or chicken.

1 tinned red pimento
1.5 dl ($\frac{1}{4}$ pint) home-made
  mayonnaise (see page
  147)
2 tablespoons tomato
  purée (use concentrated
tomato purée from a
tube or the home-made
variety on page 162)
salt and freshly ground
  black pepper

Drain the red pimento and roughly chop the flesh. Combine the mayonnaise, tomato purée and red pimento in the Magimix bowl, season with salt and pepper and process until the ingredients are well mixed and the pimento is finely chopped.

151

Mousseline verte

A cold mousseline flavoured and coloured with spinach; excellent to serve with fish.

1.5 dl (¼ pint) home-made mayonnaise (see page 147)

1 tablespoon spinach purée
2 tablespoons double cream
salt and white pepper

USE THE
METAL BLADE

Combine the mayonnaise, spinach and cream in the Magimix bowl, season with salt and pepper and process until thick and light.

Magimix vinaigrette

If you want to make a really good salad dressing just stirring the ingredients is not enough – they must be really well mixed. By using your Magimix food processor to process the ingredients you will be able to obtain a vinaigrette dressing that will perform miracles for even the most simple of salads and by using this basic vinaigrette you can produce the most exotic variations by adding herbs, spices or other ingredients.

1 teaspoon Dijon mustard or ½ teaspoon dry English mustard
salt and freshly ground black pepper

small pinch sugar
1 small clove garlic
3 tablespoons white wine or red wine vinegar
9 tablespoons olive oil

USE THE
METAL BLADE

Combine all the ingredients in the Magimix bowl and process until well blended and slightly thickened.

Variations

1. Add a little blue or Stilton cheese to the ingredients.
2. Process some parsley, chervil or chives or a combination of herbs until finely chopped before adding the ingredients for the basic vinaigrette dressing.
3. Process some red pepper until finely chopped before adding the ingredients for the vinaigrette dressing.
4. Process some crisply fried bacon until it is finely chopped before adding the ingredients for the basic vinaigrette dressing.
5. Add some grated Cheddar cheese to the basic vinaigrette dressing.

152

6. Add 15 ml (1 tablespoon) tomato ketchup and a few drops of Tabasco sauce to the ingredients for the basic dressing before processing.

7. Add a roughly chopped hard-boiled egg to the processed vinaigrette dressing and continue to process until the hard-boiled egg is finely chopped.

Curried vinaigrette dressing

A spicey dressing that goes well with potato and other slightly bland ingredients.

5 tablespoons olive oil
1½ tablespoons cider or
   white wine vinegar
¼ teaspoon Dijon mustard

1 teaspoon curry powder
1 teaspoon lemon juice
salt and freshly ground
   black pepper

USE THE
PLASTIC BLADE

Combine all the ingredients in the Magimix bowl and process until the ingredients are well mixed and slightly thickened. Store the dressing in a screw-top jar in the refrigerator.

Russian dressing

Serve with a mixed salad of vegetables.

1 egg
1 teaspoon dry mustard
1 tablespoon white wine
   vinegar
¼ teaspoon lemon juice
salt and freshly ground
   black pepper

3 dl (½ pint) olive oil
2 tablespoons tomato
   ketchup
1 teaspoon horseradish
   sauce

USE THE
PLASTIC
BLADE

Place the egg, mustard, vinegar and lemon juice in the Magimix bowl and season with salt and freshly ground black pepper. Process until the ingredients are well blended. With the machine still going, gradually pour in the oil, in a thin steady stream, through the feed tube and process until the mixture thickens and the oil has been used up. Add the tomato ketchup and the horseradish sauce and process for just long enough to blend the ingredients.

Hazelnut salad dressing

Use only fresh hazelnuts for this dressing or it will have a slightly stale flavour. It goes well with a green salad of lamb's lettuce, chicory or watercress.

37 g (1½ oz) shelled
   hazelnuts
salt and freshly ground
   black pepper

juice of 1 lemon
100 g (4 oz) single cream
a pinch of sugar

USE THE
METAL BLADE
Place the hazelnuts in the Magimix bowl and process until the nuts are very finely chopped. Add the salt and pepper, lemon juice, cream and a pinch of sugar and process until the ingredients are just mixed.

Honey dressing

Try this dressing over very thin slices of cucumber and let them marinade for a few hours in the sauce.

1½ teaspoons thick honey
4 leaves fresh majoram or
   pinch dried majoram
1 tablespoon lemon juice

1 tablespoon cider vinegar
4 tablespoons olive oil
salt and freshly ground
   black pepper

USE THE
METAL BLADE
Combine all the ingredients in the Magimix bowl, season with salt and pepper and process until they are well mixed.

Vinaigrette Noix

A most superior salad dressing. The best salad dressings in the world are made with pure walnut oil but since walnut oil is both difficult to find in this country and very expensive even if you can find it, I have found the most excellent substitute by processing walnuts in the Magimix and giving a delicious walnut flavour to the dressing together with an unusual texture that goes well with almost any salad.

Do use good olive oil. I buy olive oil whenever I am on the Continent. It weighs a lot but at least the Customs don't count the number of bottles you bring home.

4 walnuts, shelled
1 small garlic clove
1 teaspoon Dijon mustard
4 tablespoons olive oil

1 tablespoon white wine
vinegar or lemon juice
salt and freshly ground
black pepper

USE THE
METAL BLADE
Put the walnuts into the Magimix bowl with the garlic clove and process for just a few seconds until the walnuts are very finely chopped. Add the remaining ingredients to the walnut, switch on the Magimix and process for a further 10 seconds until all the ingredients are amalgamated.

Pour the dressing over your salad at the last minute before serving and toss lightly to coat the ingredients.

Ravigote dressing

Serve with globe artichokes, prawns or a green salad.

2 sprigs parsley, chives and
tarragon
1 hard-boiled egg
8 tablespoons olive oil

3 tablespoons white wine
vinegar
1 tablespoon capers
salt and freshly ground
black pepper

Remove the stalks from the herbs. Roughly chop the egg.

USE THE
METAL BLADE
Place the herbs in the Magimix bowl and process until the herbs are finely chopped. Add the remaining ingredients, season with salt and black pepper and process until the capers and hard-boiled egg are finely chopped.

Cream cheese dressing

Serve with cold asparagus, a cold bean salad or a bacon and spinach salad.

1 small bunch chervil
75 g (3 oz) cream cheese
1 teaspoon salt
pinch paprika pepper

1 tablespoon lemon juice
1 egg yolk
4 tablespoons olive oil

Remove the stalks from the chervil.

USE THE
METAL BLADE
Place the chervil in the Magimix bowl and process until finely chopped. Add the cream cheese, salt, paprika, lemon juice and egg yolk and process until ingredients are smooth. With the machine running add the oil in a thin steady stream through the feed tube.

155

Sauce verte

Bring 3 dl ($\frac{1}{2}$ pint) water to boiling point and throw in 8 spinach leaves, 25 g (1 oz) watercress, 1 spring onion, 1 tablespoon fresh tarragon leaves and 1 tablespoon fresh parsley leaves. Boil for 3 minutes, drain well and pat dry with kitchen paper. Cool. Place the leaves in the Magimix bowl and process until smooth before adding the egg yolks and continuing in the same way as mayonnaise.

Salsa verte

The classic Italian green sauce that makes so much difference to the flavour of so many of their pasta and vegetable dishes. It used to involve a long preparation of pounding in a mortar but now it can be made in only seconds in your Magimix food processor, and is a sauce I make frequently when I have fresh basil on my kitchen windowsill.

3 cloves garlic
3 sprigs basil
4 walnuts

30 ml (2 tablespoons) olive
oil

Peel and roughly chop the garlic.

USE THE
METAL BLADE

Combine the garlic, basil, walnuts and olive oil in the Magimix bowl and process until the ingredients are reduced to a smooth purée.

Pistou

If you have access to fresh basil or grow it on your windowsill (not difficult to do) this classic Italian sauce is invaluable for many dishes. Serve it by itself over spaghetti or incorporate it into a soup.

4 sprigs fresh basil
50 g (2 oz) Parmesan
cheese
3 tablespoons olive oil
6 shelled walnuts
1 tablespoon pine kernels
2 cloves garlic

salt and freshly ground
black pepper
2 tablespoons warm water
(preferably water in
which pasta has been
cooked)

Roughly chop the basil

156

Place the basil in the Magimix bowl and process until the basil is finely chopped. Add the Parmesan cheese, roughly broken up and continue to process until the cheese and basil are reduced to a paste. Add the olive oil, walnuts, pine kernels and garlic and process until the mixture is reduced to a paste. Season with salt and freshly ground black pepper and add the warm water. Switch on and off to mix the ingredients.

Pistou with gruyère, parsley and tomato

75 g (3 oz) Gruyère cheese
1 small bunch parsley
10 basil leaves
6 cloves garlic

1 tablespoon tomato paste
4 tablespoons olive oil
salt and freshly ground
black pepper

Grate the Gruyère cheese through the grating disc and remove from the bowl.
Remove the stalks from the parsley.

Combine the parsley and basil in the Magimix bowl and process until the herbs are finely chopped. Add the garlic, tomato paste and olive oil and process until the mixture is reduced to a purée. Add the cheese, season with salt and freshly ground black pepper and process for just long enough to mix the ingredients.

Sauce hollandaise

4 egg yolks
1 tablespoon water
2 tablespoons lemon juice

175 g (6 oz) melted butter
salt and freshly ground
black pepper

Place the egg yolks, water and lemon juice in the Magimix bowl and process until light and well mixed. With the machine switched on, add the melted butter through the feed tube in a slow, steady, stream and continue to process for 30 seconds.
Transfer the sauce to a double boiler and cook over hot, not boiling, water stirring continually until the sauce has the consistency of a custard.
If the sauce is not to be served at once, keep it warm by

standing it in a bowl over warm water and covering the top tightly with foil.

Note Should the sauce curdle whilst it is cooking (this is usually due to not stirring enough during the cooking process or to allowing the water below the double boiler to boil, return it to the Magimix bowl, switch on and add 1–2 tablespoons of boiling water through the feed tube, a little at a time.

Sauce mousseline

sauce hollandaise recipe   *4 tablespoons double cream*

Make the hollandaise sauce and leave it in the Magimix bowl. Whip the cream until thick. Add the cream to the hollandaise sauce, switch the machine on and off to incorporate the cream into the sauce and serve at once.

Sauce maltaise

Follow the directions for making a sauce hollandaise and mix in 1 tablespoon orange juice and 1 teaspoon finely grated orange peel. Switch the machine on and off to incorporate the ingredients just before serving.

Tomato sauce

This is a sauce I find invaluable. No trouble at all to make, it provides interest and extra flavour to a wide variety of dishes from the most mundane fish fingers to a sophisticated fillet of lamb wrapped in a pastry case.

1 large onion
1–2 cloves garlic
1 tablespoon olive or
  vegetable oil
1 tin tomatoes, approx
  425 g (15 oz)
1.5 dl ($\frac{1}{4}$ pint) water
1 tablespoon tomato purée

$\frac{1}{2}$ teaspoon mixed dried
  oregano, majoram and
  sage
1 bay leaf
salt and freshly ground
  black pepper
pinch sugar.

Peel and roughly chop the onion and garlic.

USE THE
METAL BLADE

Place the onion and garlic in the Magimix bowl and process until the onion is finely chopped.

158

Heat the oil in a saucepan. Add the onion and garlic and cook over a low heat until the onion is soft and transparent. Add the tomatoes, water, purée and herbs, season with salt, pepper and a pinch of sugar, bring to the boil, cover and simmer for 30 minutes.

Remove the bay leaf and transfer the sauce to the Magimix bowl and process until smooth.

Variations

Use red or white wine in the place of the water.

Add the grated rind of 1 orange to the sauce.

Add 1 peeled and chopped carrot to the sauce with the tomatoes to give a thicker texture.

Add some finely chopped, fresh basil to the finished sauce.

Sauce Dumas

1 large tin tomatoes
2 sprigs parsley and chervil
1 teaspoon white wine
   vinegar
1 tablespoon made English
   mustard

salt and freshly ground
   black pepper
2 tablespoons olive oil
$\frac{1}{2}$ small shallot

Turn the tomatoes into a saucepan and cook over a low heat, uncovered, until the juice has evaporated. Mash the tomatoes with a fork and continue to cook until they have been reduced to a thick purée. Leave to cool.

USE THE
METAL BLADE

Place the parsley and chervil leaves in the Magimix bowl and process until the herbs are finely chopped. Add the tomatoes and vinegar and continue to process until the tomatoes are smooth. Add the mustard, season with salt and pepper and with the machine switched on, add the oil, drop by drop, through the feed tube. When all the oil has been used up, switch off the machine, add the shallot, cut into four, to the sauce and process for just long enough for the shallot to be finely chopped.

Serve cold with fish, chicken or hard-boiled eggs.

Onion sauce

A beautifully flavoured and creamy sauce to serve with poached eggs, chicken, veal or lamb. It also makes a good covering for cooked vegetables – sprinkle the vegetables with cheese and brown in a hot oven before serving.

225 g (8 oz) onions
37 g (1¼ oz) butter
1½ tablespoons flour
3 dl (½ pint) boiling milk

salt and white pepper
pinch grated nutmeg
2 tablespoons double
  cream

USE THE
SLICING DISC
Peel the onions and slice them through the slicing disc.
   Melt the butter in a heavy pan, add the onions and cook over a low heat, with a cover on, for 15 minutes until very soft (check to see the onions are not browning – they should be pale and transparent and not coloured in any way). Add the flour and mix well. Gradually blend in the hot milk stirring over a medium high heat until the sauce comes to the boil and is thick and smooth.

USE THE
METAL BLADE
Transfer the sauce to the Magimix bowl, season with salt, pepper and nutmeg and process until smooth. Reheat and blend in the cream before serving.

Gooseberry sauce

Traditionally served with fried or grilled mackerel.

225 g (8 oz) green
  gooseberries
2 tablespoons water

pinch mixed spice
25 g (1 oz) butter
25 g (1 oz) sugar

Top and tail the gooseberries and combine them in a saucepan with the water and mixed spice. Bring to the boil, cover and simmer until the gooseberries are tender – for about 10 minutes.

USE THE
METAL BLADE
Transfer the gooseberry mixture to the Magimix bowl and add the butter and sugar. Process for just a few seconds until the fruit is puréed. Check the tartness of the sauce and add a little extra sugar if necessary but the sauce should have a bit of a bite to it or you might find it a bit sickly with the rich fish.

160

Cranberry sauce

Serve with roast turkey, roast chicken or roast game.

225 g (8 oz) cranberries
225 g (8 oz) granulated
  sugar

1.5 dl (¼ pint) water
2 tablespoons port
pinch thyme

Combine the cranberries, sugar and water in a saucepan, bring to the boil, cover and simmer for 10 minutes.

USE THE
METAL BLADE

Transfer the cranberry mixture to the Magimix bowl, add the port and thyme and process until smooth.

Green tomato chutney

1.35 kg (3 lb) unpeeled
  green tomatoes
900 g (2 lb) cooking apples
100 g (4 oz) preserved
  ginger
675 g (1½ lb) onions

100 g (4 oz) seedless
  raisins
450 g (1 lb) soft brown
  sugar
4.5 dl (¾ pint) malt vinegar
2¼ teaspoons salt

Quarter the tomatoes. Peel, core and roughly chop the apples. Roughly chop the ginger. Peel and quarter the onions.

USE THE
METAL BLADE

Half fill the Magimix bowl with tomatoes and process until the tomatoes are coarsely chopped. Remove the tomatoes to a large saucepan and process the rest.

Half fill the Magimix bowl with the apples and process until coarsely chopped. Add the apples to the tomatoes, process the rest of the apples and mix tomatoes and apples together.

Half fill the Magimix bowl with the onions and process until the onions are coarsely chopped. Remove and process the remaining onions. Add the processed onions to the tomatoes and apples. Place the ginger in the Magimix bowl and process until finely chopped. Mix the ginger and raisins into the other ingredients with the sugar, vinegar and salt. Bring to the boil over a high heat stirring every now and then. Reduce the heat and simmer, uncovered, for 3 hours until the liquid has been absorbed by the chutney. Stir frequently to prevent the ingredients sticking.

161

Spoon the chutney into hot, dry jars leaving 3 mm ($\frac{1}{8}$ in.) clearance at the top of the jars. Cover with a circle of wax paper or cellophane and screw the lids on tightly. Store in a cool, dark place.

Home-made tomato purée

Infinitely preferable to the commercial paste that comes from a tin or tube. This purée is full of flavour and has that individual touch that only you can supply to food. The purée is strong and rich and only needs to be added in small quantities to give the required tomato and herb flavouring. Store it in a screw top jar in a refrigerator for up to one week or keep it in the deep freeze (I freeze mine in ice cube containers) for up to three months and use as required.

Add the purée to home-made mayonnaise to make a rich sauce for a fish salad or prawn cocktail. Colour sour cream to be used as a garnish with a teaspoon of the purée. Add some of the purée to a white sauce that has been made with chicken stock and produce a delicious, quick sauce to go with a roast or grilled chicken.

1 large onion
2 cloves garlic
1 large tin tomatoes
   (575 g/1 lb 4 oz)
1½ tablespoons olive oil
1 teaspoon grated orange
   peel
½ teaspoon mixed dried
   oregano, thyme, savory
   and basil
1 bay leaf
salt and freshly ground
   black pepper
2 teaspoons sugar
few drops Tabasco sauce

Peel and roughly chop the onion. Peel the garlic cloves. Rub the tomatoes through a food mill or a sieve to remove the pips.

USE THE
METAL BLADE

Place the onion and garlic in the Magimix bowl and process until the onion is finely chopped.

Heat the oil in a saucepan. Add the onion and garlic and cook over a low heat until the onion is soft and transparent. Add the remaining ingredients, bring to the boil and simmer for 20 minutes over a medium heat, stirring every now and then.

162

Turn the mixture into the Magimix bowl and process until it is reduced to a smooth purée. Return the purée to a clean saucepan bring to the boil and cook over a high heat, stirring occasionally, until the purée is reduced to a thick, richly red paste (there should be about half the quantity you started with).

Spoon the purée into a screw-topped jar and store in the refrigerator.

Sauce espagnole

A well flavoured basic brown sauce that is used in many dishes and as the basis of more sophisticated sauces.

1 small onion
1 small carrot
50 g (2 oz) lean bacon
1 celery stalk
37 g (1½ oz) dripping or
  butter
25 g (1 oz) flour
½ tablespoon tomato purée

4.5 dl (¾ pint) brown stock
1 bay leaf
1 sprig parsley
1 small sprig thyme
salt and freshly ground
  black pepper
1 tablespoon Madeira or
  medium dry sherry.

Peel and quarter the onion. Peel and roughly chop the carrot. Remove the rinds from the bacon and roughly chop the rashers. Roughly chop the celery stalk.

Place the bacon in the Magimix bowl and process until the bacon is fairly finely chopped. Add the onion, carrot and celery and process until the vegetables are finely chopped.

Melt the dripping or butter in a saucepan, add the vegetables and bacon and cook over a low heat for 5 minutes, stirring to prevent sticking, until the vegetables are soft. Add the flour and continue to cook over a low heat, stirring, until the flour is coloured to a hazelnut brown. Add the tomato purée and mix well. Gradually blend in the stock, stirring continually over a medium high heat until the sauce comes to the boil and is thick and smooth. Add the herbs, tied in a bundle, season with salt and pepper and simmer, covered, for 1 hour. Remove the herbs and return the sauce to the Magimix bowl. Process until smooth and return to a clean pan. Heat through and mix in the Madeira or sherry.

Note It is worth keeping a portion or two of this sauce in your deep freeze for emergencies.

163

Sauce chasseur

Follow the directions for making a sauce espagnole but substitute white wine for half the stock. Add 50 g (2 oz) of firm button mushrooms, sliced through the Magimix slicing disc and lightly sautéed in 12 g ($\frac{1}{2}$ oz) butter to the finished sauce with $\frac{1}{2}$ tablespoon of mixed fresh finely chopped parsley, chervil and tarragon (the herbs can be chopped with the metal blade in a clean bowl).

Swiss cheese fondue

Serves 4

1 clove garlic
450 g (1 lb) Gruyère cheese
1 teaspoon cornflour
1 glass Kirsch
2 glasses dry white wine

12 g ($\frac{1}{4}$ oz) butter
thick slices of white bread
    with the crusts removed,
    cut into bite-sized pieces

Peel the garlic clove and rub it around the bottom and sides of a flameproof, earthenware casserole.

USE THE
GRATING DISC

Grate the cheese through the grating disc. Mix the cornflour with the Kirsch.

Place the cheese in the casserole with the wine and put over a spirit lamp. Heat over a medium flame, stirring continually until the cheese melts and the fondue is thick and smooth. Add the Kirsch and the butter to the cheese and wine, mix well and stir over a medium heat for 2 minutes. Turn the heat right down to keep the fondue warm while it is being eaten.

The pieces of bread are speared onto the ends of long forks, dipped into the fondue mixture and eaten from the ends of the forks.

Sauce piquante

A delicious light sauce to serve with hot asparagus or other vegetables.

1 small bunch parsley
1 small onion
100 g (4 oz) butter
1 tablespoon flour
3 dl ($\frac{1}{2}$ pint) chicken stock

2 bay leaves
salt and freshly ground
   black pepper
3 egg yolks
juice of $\frac{1}{2}$ a lemon

Remove the stalks from the parsley. Peel and halve the onion.

USE THE
METAL BLADE

Place the parsley leaves in the Magimix bowl and process until the leaves are finely chopped. The parsley can be left in the bowl.

USE THE JUICE
EXTRACTOR

Process the onion through the juice extractor to extract the juice.
   Melt the butter in a saucepan. Add the flour and mix well. Gradually blend in the chicken stock, stirring continually over a medium high heat until the sauce is thick and smooth. Add the bay leaves, parsley and onion juice and season with salt and freshly ground black pepper. Bring to the boil and simmer for 6 minutes.

USE THE
METAL BLADE

Remove the bay leaves from the sauce and transfer the hot sauce to the Magimix bowl. With the machine switched on, add the egg yolks, one by one, processing until each yolk has been well mixed into the sauce. Add the lemon juice, process for just long enough to mix and serve the sauce as quickly as possible.
   Note If necessary the sauce can be reheated in a double boiler over hot water but it should not be allowed to cook.

Mixed herb butter

1 small bunch parsley
1 small bunch chives

57–85 g (2–3 oz) softened
   butter
salt and white pepper

Remove the coarse stalks from the parsley and roughly chop the chives.

165

Place the parsley leaves and chives in the Magimix bowl and process until the herbs are finely chopped. Add the butter, season with salt and pepper and continue to process until the mixture is smooth and the herbs are well mixed into the butter. Shape the butter into a sausage on foil and roll up neatly. Chill the butter in the refrigerator until firm and then cut into half inch thick slices.

Serve on grilled fish, poultry or meat.

Duxelles

This is a classic French preparation used in many dishes. It is half way between the consistency of a stuffing and a sauce and can be invaluable as a flavouring ingredient.

1 small bunch parsley (4 sprigs)	1 dessertspoon tomato purée
1 onion, peeled and quartered	4 tablespoons water
100 g (4 oz) firm button mushrooms	2 tablespoons dry white wine
25 g (1 oz) butter	1 teaspoon sugar
pinch rosemary	salt and freshly ground black pepper

Remove the stalks of the parsley and put the heads in the Magimix bowl. Process until the parsley is finely chopped. Remove the parsley. Put the onion in the Magimix bowl and process until finely chopped. Remove the onion. Put the mushrooms in the Magimix bowl and process until mushrooms are finely chopped.

Melt the butter in a small pan. Add the onion and cook over a low heat until the onion is soft and transparent. Add the mushrooms and cook for a further minute. Add the parsley, rosemary, tomato purée, water, white wine and sugar and season with salt and freshly ground black pepper. Mix well and simmer for 2 minutes.

Stilton butter

57 g (2 oz) Stilton cheese	57–85 g (2–3 oz) softened butter

Combine the butter and Stilton cheese in the Magimix bowl and process until smooth and well mixed.

166

Shape the butter into a sausage on a piece of foil and roll up neatly. Chill the butter in the refrigerator until firm and cut then cut into half inch thick slices.

Serve on fried or grilled hamburgers, steaks or on grilled fish cutlets.

Savoury garlic butter

1 sprig parsley
1 shallot
2 cloves garlic

57–85 g (2–3 oz) softened
butter
salt and pepper

Remove the stalk from the parsley. Peel and roughly chop the shallot. Peel and roughly chop the garlic.

USE THE
METAL BLADE

Combine the parsley, shallot and garlic in the Magimix bowl and process until the shallot is finely chopped. Add the butter, season with a little salt and pepper and continue to process until the mixture is smooth.

Use the butter as a stuffing for snails or for stuffing and baking mushroom caps.

Sweet and sour sauce

2.5 cm (1 in.) piece green
ginger, peeled
1 medium onion
1 small green pepper
2 tablespoons vegetable oil
4 tablespoons brown sugar
2 tablespoons cornflour

1.5 dl ($\frac{1}{4}$ pint) white wine
or cider vinegar
3 tablespoons soy sauce
1 tablespoon tomato purée
4.5 dl ($\frac{3}{4}$ pint) chicken
stock

Roughly chop the ginger. Peel the onion. Remove the seeds and core of the green pepper and roughly chop the flesh.

USE THE
METAL BLADE

Place the ginger root in the Magimix bowl and process until the ginger is very finely chopped. Add the pepper and continue to process until the pepper is coarsely chopped. Remove the ginger and pepper.

167

USE THE
SLICING DISC Slice the onion through the slicing disc. Remove the onion.

USE THE
METAL BLADE Combine the sugar, cornflour, vinegar and soy sauce in the Magimix bowl and process until the ingredients are well mixed and smooth. Add $\frac{1}{4}$ of the stock and process for 20 seconds. Heat the oil in a saucepan. Add the ginger and pepper and the onion slices and cook over a medium heat for 3 minutes. Add the liquid from the Magimix bowl, stir in the remaining stock and bring to the boil stirring all the time until the sauce is thick, clear and shining.

Lemon and parsley butter

Serve with chicken, fish or steaks.

1 bunch parsley
100 g (4 oz) butter
1 tablespoon lemon juice

1 tablespoon double
* (heavy) cream*
salt and freshly ground
* black pepper*

USE THE
METAL BLADE Remove the parsley stalks. Roughly cut up the butter. Place the parsley leaves in the Magimix bowl and process until the parsley is finely chopped. Add the lemon juice, butter and cream and season with a little salt and plenty of freshly ground black pepper. Process until ingredients are smooth.

Home made peanut butter

Freshly made peanut butter has a definite edge over commercial products. By adding a few extra peanuts at the end of the processing procedure you can give an extra crunchy texture.

227 g ($\frac{1}{2}$ lb) salted peanuts

2 teaspoons groundnut or
* vegetable oil*

USE THE
METAL BLADE Combine the peanuts and oil in the Magimix bowl and process until the mixture is reduced to a smooth paste. Add some extra peanuts to the paste to give extra crunch and process for just long enough to chop the extra nuts.

Beurre mousseux

A light whipped butter sauce to serve with poached or baked fish.

1 small bunch parsley
1 sprig tarragon
225 g (8 oz) butter
105 ml (3½ fl. oz) fish stock

105 ml (3½ fl. oz) lemon
*   juice*
salt and freshly ground
*   black pepper*

Remove the stalks from the parsley and tarragon.
Leave the butter to stand at room temperature for 30 minutes.

USE THE
METAL BLADE
Place the herbs in the Magimix bowl and process until the herbs are finely chopped. Remove the herbs.
Roughly chop the butter and place it in the Magimix bowl. Process until the butter is soft and smooth. With the motor running, gradually add the fish stock and the lemon juice processing until the mixture is light and creamy. Season with salt and pepper and the herbs and switch on and off to incorporate the seasoning and the herbs.

Sauce aux crevettes

The secret of this sauce is to chop the mushrooms after they have been sautéed in butter.

50 g (2 oz) shelled prawns
56 g (2¼ oz) butter
100 g (4 oz) button
*   mushrooms*
2 tablespoons flour

3 dl (½ pint) milk
1 tablespoon tomato purée
salt and white pepper
2 tablespoons double cream

USE THE
METAL BLADE
Place the prawns in the Magimix bowl and process until roughly chopped. Remove the prawns.
Melt 1 oz butter in a saucepan. Add the mushrooms and cook over a medium heat for 4 minutes. Drain the mushrooms and cook over a medium heat for 4 minutes. Drain the mushrooms thoroughly and place them in the Magimix bowl. Process until the mushrooms are finely chopped.
Melt the remaining butter in a saucepan. Add the flour and mix well. Gradually blend in the milk, stirring continually until the sauce comes to the boil and is thick and

smooth. Add the tomato purée and simmer slowly for 5 minutes. Mix in the mushrooms and prawns, season with salt and pepper and blend in the cream just before serving.

Note The mushrooms must be well drained or the sauce will have an unattractive grey colouring to it.

Butterscotch and walnut sauce

Serve with vanilla, chocolate or coffee ice cream.

37 g (1½ oz) shelled walnuts
50 g (2 oz) butter
50 g (2 oz) soft brown sugar

1 tablespoon golden syrup
grated rind and juice of 1 lemon

Toast the walnuts in a hot oven for about 2 minutes until crisp.

USE THE METAL BLADE

Process the walnuts in the Magimix bowl until fairly finely chopped.

Combine the butter, sugar and golden syrup in a small heavy pan and cook over a low heat, stirring every now and then, until the butter is melted and the sauce comes to the boil. Boil over a high heat without stirring for about 3 minutes until the syrup turns a dark golden brown and becomes thick and creamy. Remove the sauce from the heat and beat in the lemon peel and lemon juice. Add the walnuts, mix well and serve hot.

Egg custard sauce

Quite a different thing altogether from the powdered custard and delicious to serve with those hot, old-fashioned steamed puddings.

2 eggs
1 tablespoon caster sugar

3 dl (½ pint) milk
2 drops vanilla essence

USE THE METAL BLADE

Combine the eggs and sugar in the Magimix bowl and process until the mixture is smooth (do not over-process or the mixture will froth up). Heat the milk to just below boiling point and, with the motor running, add the milk

170

through the feed tube and switch off the motor. Add the vanilla essence. Switch on and off to mix the ingredients and transfer the custard to a clean, heavy pan. Cook over a very low heat, stirring continually, until the custard thickens enough to coat the back of a wooden spoon.

Note The heat should be really low to prevent the custard scrambling and this process can sometimes take as long as 8 minutes – you have to be patient.

Dips made with the Magimix food processor

Quickly made, well flavoured dips can be a boon to any housewife. I once found myself demonstrating a Magimix food processor at a large Christmas fair. An enormous crowd pressed around my stand, craning their necks and pushing forward as I tried to compete against the noise of dancing to Hungarian music and the banging and drilling that accompanied some alterations which were being made to the hall in which the fair was taking place.

It was impossible to please all my fascinated onlookers and although I worked magic with pastry, ground up beef by the pound, conjured up pâtés in a flash and made goodness knows how many Christmas cakes, those at the back complained they couldn't see and those in the middle were so fascinated that most of them stayed there all day.

I discovered, half way through the day, how to keep the whole audience happy. Between zipping out my pâtés, quiches and other Magimix musts, I whizzed up dips in just seconds and had a couple of helpers pass them round with small biscuits. I didn't follow any definite recipe, merely threw in a mixture of ingredients I thought would blend well together. Each time the effect was electric. My audience could not believe dips could be made quite so quickly and fortunately each one seemed to taste better than the last; what is more this mini testing kept everyone happy and made the demonstration go with a real swing.

Experiment with various ingredients to make your own dips and serve them with small salted biscuits or with thin strips of raw carrot, celery or green pepper or with florettes of cauliflower.

171

A Good Magimix Dip

small bunch chives
3 tablespoons mayonnaise
1.5 dl ($\frac{1}{4}$ pint) tomato juice
100 g (4 oz) cream cheese

$\frac{1}{4}$ teaspoon Worcestershire
 sauce
1 tablespoon sweet pickle

USE THE
METAL BLADE

Make sure the bowl is dry before processing the chives.
Roughly chop the chives, put them into the Magimix bowl
and process until the chives are finely chopped. Switch
off, add the remaining ingredients to the bowl and continue to process until the ingredients are well mixed.
Serve chilled.

Avocado dip

2 stalks celery
50 g (2 oz) mixed salted
 nuts
1 avocado

1 teaspoon lime or lemon
 juice
salt and freshly ground
 black pepper
2 drops Tabasco sauce

USE THE
METAL BLADE

Roughly chop the celery and put the stalks into the
Magimix bowl with the nuts. Process until the mixture is
reduced to a smooth paste. Peel and roughly chop the
avocado and add it to the ingredients in the Magimix bowl
with the lime or lemon juice, seasoning and Tabasco sauce.
Process until well blended.

Pile the mixture onto a serving dish or into a bowl and
serve well chilled.

Tapenade

An exciting Spanish dip for use as a dip with crudités.

8 anchovy fillets
1 small tin tuna fish
 (200 g/7 oz)
18 black olives with the
 stones removed

1.5 dl ($\frac{1}{4}$ pint) olive oil
2 tablespoons brandy
1 teaspoon lemon juice
freshly ground black pepper

USE THE
METAL BLADE

Combine the ingredients in the Magimix bowl and process until the mixture is reduced to a thick mayonnaise-
like consistency. Season with freshly ground black pepper

and switch the machine on and off to incorporate the seasoning.

Serve chilled.

Bagna cauda

A richly flavoured Italian dip to serve with crudités.

4 cloves garlic	*8 fillets anchovy*
1.5 dl (5 fl. oz) olive oil	*1 teaspoon lemon juice*
37 g (1½ oz) butter	*freshly ground black pepper*

Peel and roughly chop the garlic.

USE THE
METAL BLADE

Combine all the ingredients in the Magimix bowl and process until reduced to a smooth paste. Season with freshly ground black pepper and switch on and off to incorporate the seasoning.

Turn the mixture into a heavy saucepan and cook over a low heat stirring all the time until the mixture is thick and creamy.

Serve warm.

Sandwich fillings

Cheese and lettuce filling with onion

6 lettuce leaves	*1 small onion*
100 g (4 oz) Cheddar cheese	*1 tablespoon mayonnaise*

Wash the lettuce leaves and pat them dry with kitchen paper. Tear the leaves into shreds.

USE THE
GRATING DISC

Break the cheese into pieces and grate through the grating disc. Remove the cheese.

USE THE
SLICING DISC

Peel and halve the onion lengthwise. Slice the onion through the slicing disc.

Butter slices of white bread. Sprinkle some grated cheese on half the slices, place a few onion rings on top of the cheese and finish off with the lettuce. Spread some mayonnaise on the other slices of bread and place them on top of the sandwich.

173

Marmite and cheese filling

100 g (4 oz) Cheddar
  cheese
2 teaspoons Marmite

buttered slices of brown
  bread

USE THE
GRATING DISC

Break the cheese into pieces and grate the cheese through the grating disc. Thinly spread Marmite on buttered slices of brown bread, sprinkle with grated cheese and top with another slice of buttered bread.

Anchovy and cheese filling

4 anchovy fillets
yolks of 2 hard-boiled eggs
75 g (3 oz) cream cheese

salt and freshly ground
  black pepper

USE THE
METAL BLADE

Combine the anchovy fillets, egg yolks and cream cheese in the Magimix bowl and season with a little salt and freshly ground black pepper. Spread on buttered slices of brown bread.

Grated celery and apple filling

1 crisp eating apple
1 stick celery

4 tablespoons mayonnaise
salt and white pepper

Peel, core and roughly chop the apple. Trim the celery.

USE THE
GRATING DISC

Grate the apple and celery through the grating disc. Combine the apple and celery with the mayonnaise to bind and season with a little salt and pepper. Spread on buttered slices of bread.

Sardine filling

1 shallot
1 tin sardines
37 g (1½ oz) softened
  butter

salt and freshly ground
  black pepper

Peel and quarter the shallot. Drain the sardines.

USE THE
METAL BLADE

Put the shallot in the Magimix bowl and process until finely chopped. Add the sardines and butter, season with salt and pepper and turn the machine on until the mixture is reduced to a smooth paste.

Cream cheese, olive and pepper filling

6 black olives
¼ green pepper
50 g (2 oz) cream cheese

2 tablespoons double cream
1 teaspoon lemon juice
salt

USE THE
METAL BLADE

Remove the stones from the olives. Remove any seeds from the pepper and roughly chop the flesh. Combine the olives and pepper in the Magimix bowl and process until finely chopped. Add the cream cheese, cream and lemon juice, season with a little salt and switch the machine on and off to mix the ingredients.

Chicken and roast almond

37 g (1½ oz) slivered or
  nibbed almonds
100 g (4 oz) cooked
  chicken

1 tablespoon curry powder
1.5 dl (¼ pint) mayonnaise

Roast the almonds in a hot oven until crisp and golden brown (3 minutes). Leave to cool. Roughly chop the chicken.

USE THE
METAL BLADE

Place the chicken and almonds in the Magimix bowl with the curry powder and process until the chicken is finely chopped. Add the mayonnaise and switch on and off to mix the ingredients.

175

Bacon and mushroom

One of the most delicious fillings. Serve it hot in a toasted sandwich or cold in buttered white or brown bread.

2 rashers streaky bacon
50 g (2 oz) firm button
   mushrooms

freshly ground black pepper
12 g ($\frac{1}{2}$ oz) butter or bacon
   fat

Remove the rinds from the bacon and finely chop the rashers.

USE THE
METAL BLADE

Place the bacon and mushrooms in the Magimix bowl and process until the ingredients are finely chopped.

Melt the butter in a frying pan, add the bacon and mushrooms and cook over a medium heat, stirring every now and then, for 3–5 minutes until the ingredients are cooked. Season with salt and pepper and use hot or cold.

Egg spread

4 hard-boiled eggs
2 spring onions
1.5 dl ($\frac{1}{4}$ pint) mayonnaise

salt and freshly ground
   black pepper

USE THE
METAL BLADE

Peel and halve the eggs. Roughly chop the spring onions. Place the eggs, spring onions and mayonnaise in the Magimix bowl and season with salt and freshly ground black pepper. Process until the eggs are finely chopped and the ingredients are well mixed.

Note For more exciting variations of this recipe, a small gherkin, some chopped ham or a little pimento can be added to the ingredients.

Peanut butter and cream cheese

4 tablespoons peanut butter
   (see page 168)

75 g (3 oz) cream cheese
50 g (2 oz) seedless raisins

USE THE
METAL BLADE

Place the ingredients in the Magimix bowl and process until the raisins are finely chopped and the ingredients are well mixed.

Pastry, cakes, biscuits, bread and batters

Basic short crust pastry

Enough for two 23 cm (9 in.) flan cases.

125 g (4½ oz) butter
40 g (1½ oz) lard
350 g (12 oz) plain flour
pinch salt

2 teaspoons sugar or salt
and pepper
1.5 dl (4–5 tablespoons) ice
cold water

Use butter and lard straight from the refrigerator and cut it into walnut sized pieces.

USE THE
METAL BLADE

Combine the butter, lard, flour and a pinch of salt in the Magimix bowl. Add sugar for a sweet pastry or a little extra salt and some white pepper for a savoury pastry. Process until the mixture is reduced to the consistency of coarse breadcrumbs.

With the machine switched on, gradually pour in the iced water through the feed tube. As soon as the dough forms a ball around the knife stop pouring in the water.

Wrap in a floured cloth or waxed paper and chill before rolling out.

177

Baking blind

Many pastry cases have to be baked 'blind' before being filled to ensure their pastry is crisp and not soggy. In the case of cold fillings the cooked pastry should be baked until crisp but when a hot filling is to be used and the dish finished in the oven, the pastry should only be half cooked before filling.

Roll out your pastry to about 3 m ($\frac{1}{8}$ in.) thickness. Line a flan dish or tartlet dishes with the pastry and lightly prick the base, all over, with a fork. Line the case with foil or greaseproof paper and fill it with special metal weights or with dried peas or beans. Bake the case in a hot oven (200°C, 400°F, Reg. 6) for 10 minutes. Remove the filling and paper or foil and continue to bake for a further 5–10 minutes.

Note Instead of lining the case with pastry the flan tin or tartlet cases can be inverted and pastry moulded over the outside of the tin. The pastry is then pricked with a fork all over and baked as above. Half way through cooking time check to see if the pastry has risen; if it has press it gently back into shape with your fingers before returning it to the oven. Cool the pastry case on the tin and then gently remove it.

Quick flaky pastry

With the Magimix food processor you will not obtain a perfect flaky pastry but a good 'quick' flaky pastry can be made in only a matter of minutes. Make sure your butter or margarine and your mixing water are really well chilled and use plenty of flour for rolling out.

350 g (12 oz) plain flour
pinch salt
225 g (8 oz) butter or
margarine

1.5 dl ($\frac{1}{4}$ pint) ice-cold
water

USE THE
METAL BLADE

Place the flour in the Magimix bowl with the salt. Add a quarter of the butter cut into small pieces and process until the mixture is reduced to the consistency of fairly fine breadcrumbs. Gradually add the water through the feed tube until the dough forms a ball around the Magimix blade. Stop the machine and pull the dough away from the centre dividing it into three pieces.

178

Cut the remaining well chilled butter or margarine into small pieces the size of peas and distribute the pieces in the Magimix bowl. Switch on the machine and process for just long enough to mix the fat into the dough.

Turn the pastry onto a floured board and roll it out to about 6 mm ($\frac{1}{4}$ in.) thick with a floured rolling pin. Fold the edges of two sides of the dough into the centre and then fold in half. Roll out again to 6 mm ($\frac{1}{4}$ in.) thickness and repeat this folling process twice more. Put the pastry into a polythene bag and chill for 30 minutes before using.

Pâté brisée

French shortcrust pastry using an egg yolk. A good pastry for all savoury and 'quiche' tarts. The quantity is enough for 24 tartlet moulds, each 5 cm (2 in.) in diameter or for a 25 cm (10 in.) flan case.

225 g (8 oz) plain flour *vegetable oil*
pinch salt *1 egg yolk*
100 g (4 oz) butter *3 tablespoons cold water*
1 tablespoon olive or

USE THE
METAL BLADE

Place the flour and salt in the Magimix bowl and add the butter cut into four pieces. Process until the mixture is reduced to the consistency of coarse breadcrumbs.

Combine the olive oil, egg yolk and water and beat lightly with a fork. With the machine switched on, add the egg mixture through the feed tube, processing until the mixture forms a ball around the knife. Switch off immediately. Chill the pastry before rolling out.

Pâté sablée

A sweet shortcrust pastry for making tarts which are to be filled with fruit. The quantity is enough for a 23–25 cm (9–10 in) flan case.

225 g (8 oz) flour *100 g (4 oz) butter*
pinch salt *1 egg yolk*
2 tablespoons caster sugar *3 tablespoons cold water*

USE THE
METAL BLADE

Combine the flour, salt and sugar in the Magimix bowl and add the butter cut into four pieces. Process until the mixture is the consistency of coarse bread crumbs.

179

Combine the egg yolk with the cold water and mix with a fork. With the machine switched on, add the egg mixture through the feed tube processing for just long eough for the dough to form a ball around the knife. Chill before rolling out.

Orange pastry

A light pastry for flans or fruit tarts with a subtle orange flavouring.

100 g (4 oz) butter
50 g (2 oz) lard
225 g (8 oz) plain flour

grated rind and juice of 1 orange

USE THE
METAL BLADE

Roughly chop the fat and place it in the Magimix bowl with the flour and orange rind. Process until the mixture is reduced to fairly fine breadcrumbs. With the machine running, add the orange juice through the feed tube processing for just long enough for the dough to form a ball around the metal blade. Chill the pastry before rolling out.

Savoury choux pastry puffs

Serves 4

The same recipe as for éclairs and profiteroles but this time with a savoury cheese flavour. Filled with a rich cream sauce, a shellfish sauce or a sauce with chicken or ham these make an ideal starter or a light lunch or supper dish.

1.5 dl ($\frac{1}{4}$ pint) water
50 g (2 oz) butter
62 g (2$\frac{1}{2}$ oz) flour

25 g (1 oz) grated
Parmesan or Cheddar
cheese
salt and cayenne pepper
2 medium eggs

Combine the water and butter and cook over a medium heat until the butter has melted and the mixture comes to the boil.

180

Place the flour and cheese in the Magimix bowl and season with salt and a pinch of cayenne pepper. Switch the Magimix food processor on and with the motor running pour the liquid mixture in a steady stream through the feed tube. Process until a smooth dough is formed. With the machine still switched on, drop in the eggs, one by one, through the feed tube processing after each egg until the mixture is smooth and shining.

Either pipe the dough through a forcing bag and a medium nozzle, in the same way as you would make éclairs, onto a lightly greased baking sheet, or drop, at generous intervals, from a teaspoon. Bake in a hot oven (220°C, 425°F, Reg. 7) for about 10–15 minutes until well puffed, golden brown and completely firm to the touch. When the puffs are ready, open the oven door and leave the puffs to settle for a minute or two to prvent them collapsing. Cool on a wire rack, cut half way through from one side and fill with the filling. The puffs can be glazed with a little aspic jelly or reheated before serving.

Cold fillings

1. Combine some cold chicken with an equal quantity of butter, seasoned with salt, pepper, a little lemon juice and a few drops of Tabasco with a flavouring of finely chopped fresh tarragon or chervil. Process in the Magimix food processor using the metal blade until the mixture is almost smooth.

2. Combine some lean and fat ham with some hot chutney, a few drops Worcestershire sauce, a little mustard and an equal quantity of butter and process in the Magimix food processor with the metal blade until smooth.

3. Process some chopped cooked tongue with a little Cumberland sauce and an equal quantity of butter to a paste in the Magimix food processor using the metal blade.

4. Fresh or smoked salmon can be mixed with half the quantity of butter, a little horseradish sauce, seasoned with salt, cayenne pepper and a little lemon juice and processed to a smooth paste in the Magimix bowl using the metal blade.

5. Process some tuna fish with an equal quantity of butter and a seasoning of salt, pepper and a little lemon juice until fairly smooth in the Magimix food processor using the metal blade.

181

Fillings for hot savoury puffs

3 dl (½ pint) milk
bay leaf
slice of onion and a blade
  of mace
25 g (1 oz) butter

25 g (1 oz) flour
50 g (2 oz) grated Cheddar
  cheese
salt and white pepper

Combine the milk, bay leaf, onion and mace in a small saucepan, bring to the boil and simmer for 3 minutes. strain the milk. Melt the butter in a saucepan, add the flour and mix well. Gradually blend in the milk, stirring continually over a medium high heat until the sauce comes to the boil and is thick and smooth. Add the cheese, season with salt and pepper and cook over a low heat for a further 3 minutes, stirring all the time until the cheese has melted.

USE THE
METAL BLADE

Transfer the sauce to the Magimix bowl, add any of the following flavouring ingredients and process for just long enough to finely chop the added ingredients. Fill the puffs with the mixture and heat through for a few minutes only in a medium hot oven until the puffs are nicely crisp and the filling is hot through.

1. Some finely chopped tarragon or chervil and some cooked chicken.

2. Some prawns and finely chopped parsley.

3. Smoked salmon and a touch of lemon juice and red pepper.

4. Fresh, cooked salmon.

Éclairs

2.25 dl (1¼ gills) water
75 g (3 oz) butter
84 g (3¾ oz) flour

3 medium eggs
whipped cream
thin chocolate icing

Combine the water and butter in a saucepan and heat over a moderate heat until the butter melts and the mixture comes to the boil.

USE THE
METAL BLADE

Place the flour in the Magimix bowl, switch on the Magimix food processor and with the motor running add the liquid, in a steady stream, through the feed tube. When the liquid has all been incorporated and the dough is smooth, with the motor still running, add the eggs, one by one, through the feed tube, processing after each addition until the dough is smooth. Process until the dough shines like silk.

Pipe the dough through a piping bag into finger shapes onto a lightly greased baking sheet leaving room for expansion and bake in a hot oven (220°C, 425°F, Reg. 7) for 10–15 minutes until the éclairs are cooked, open the oven door wide and leave the éclairs inside to settle for a minute or two before cooling on a wire rack.

Split the cooled éclairs, fill with whipped, sweetened cream and brush with a light chocolate icing.

Profiteroles

Instead of piping the choux pastry, drop it from a teaspoon in small balls and bake as above. Fill the puffs with sweetened whipped cream, pile them in a pyramid on a serving dish and pour over some melted plain chocolate thinned with a little water.

Alternative fillings

1. Fill the puffs with ice cream and serve with a hot chocolate sauce on the side.

2. Fill the profiteroles with whipped sweetened cream to which sliced strawberries have been added and brush them with icing sugar before serving.

3. Fill the profiteroles with a slightly sharp, thick apricot purée and top them with whipped cream.

Curried cheese straws

50 g (2 oz) Cheddar cheese	50 g (2 oz) butter or
100 g (4 oz) plain flour	margarine
salt	1 egg yolk
¼ teaspoon curry powder	

USE THE
GRATING DISC

Grate the Cheddar cheese through the grating disc.

USE THE
METAL BLADE

Combine the flour, a pinch of salt, the curry powder, cheese and the butter or margarine (roughly chopped) in the Magimix bowl and process until the mixture is reduced to the consistency of fine breadcrumbs. Add the egg yolk and continue to process for just long enough for the dough to form a ball around the metal blade.

Roll out the pastry to 6 mm ($\frac{1}{4}$ in.) thickness on a floured board and cut into strips 6 mm ($\frac{1}{4}$ in.) wide and 5 cm (2 in.) long. Place the strips on a greased baking sheet and bake in a hot oven (200°C, 400°F, Reg. 6) for 8–10 minutes until golden brown.

Serve warm.

Hazelnut sponge cake

50 g (2 oz) hazelnuts
75 g (3 oz) butter
75 g (3 oz) sugar
1 egg
75 g (3 oz) flour
1 teaspoon instant coffee
   dissolved in 15 ml (1
   tablespoon) hot water

2 tablespoons milk
1 level teaspoon baking
   powder
1 egg white
1.5 dl ($\frac{1}{4}$ pint double cream

USE THE
METAL BLADE

Bake the hazelnuts in a hot oven until lightly browned. Rub the nuts in a clean cloth to remove the skins and leave to cool.

Place the nuts in the Magimix bowl and process until they are very finely ground. Remove the nuts.

Cut the butter into pieces and combine the butter and sugar in the Magimix bowl. Process until the mixture is white and creamy. Add the egg, hazelnuts, flour and coffee and continue to process until well blended. Add the milk and baking powder and process briefly to mix.

Beat the egg white until very stiff and lightly fold in the hazelnut mixture. Pour into a greased and floured sandwich tin and bake in a moderate oven (180°C, 350°F, Reg. 4) for 35 minutes.

Turn the cake out onto a wire rack and leave to cool. Slice the cake in half across and fill with lightly whipped double cream.

184

Lemon cake

2 eggs
100 g (4 oz) butter
100 g (4 oz) caster sugar

grated rind and juice of 1
lemon
100 g (4 oz) self-raising
flour

Separate the eggs.

USE THE
METAL BLADE Roughly chop the butter. Combine the butter and sugar
in the Magimix bowl and process until the mixture is pale,
light and creamy.

With the machine running, drop the egg yolks through
the feed tube one at a time, processing between each
addition until the yolks are well mixed. Add the lemon
rind and lemon juice and 2 tablespoons of the flour. Continue to process until the ingredients are mixed but do not
over-process.

Whip the egg whites until very stiff. Lightly fold the
egg yolk mixture and remaining flour into the egg whites.

Pour the mixture into a greased and floured sandwich
tin and cook in a moderately hot oven (190°C, 375°F, Reg.
5) for about 25 minutes.

Serve warm, cut into slices and spread with softened
butter.

Orange and almond sponge

100 g (4 oz) blanched
almonds
100 g (4 oz) butter
100 g (4 oz) sugar
3 eggs, separated
grated rind of 1 orange

juice of 2 oranges
few drops almond essence
50 g (2 oz) plain flour
pinch salt
1 tablespoon caster sugar

USE THE
METAL BLADE Place the almonds in the Magimix bowl and process until
the almonds are reduced to a powder. Remove the
almonds.

Combine the butter and sugar in the Magimix bowl and
process until the mixture is pale yellow and creamy. With
the machine switched on, add the egg yolks, one by one
through the feed tube, processing after each addition until
the yolks are well mixed into the sugar and butter. Add

the orange rind, orange juice and a few drops of almond essence and process for just long enough to mix the ingredients. Add the almonds and flour and process until the ingredients are well mixed.

Beat the egg whites with a pinch of salt until the egg whites are stiff. Add a quarter of the egg whites to the ingredients in the Magimix bowl and switch the machine on and off quickly to lightly mix. Lightly fold the cake mixture into the remaining egg whites and pour into a well buttered and floured cake tin.

Bake the cake in a moderate oven (180°C, 350°F, Reg. 4) for 30 minutes until the cake is firm to the touch and a knitting needle plunged into the centre comes out clean.

Leave to stand for 10 minutes before turning out. Cut the cake in half across and fill the cake with butter filling (see opposite page). Sprinkle caster sugar over the top.

Chocolate cake

100 g (4 oz) unsalted
   butter
250 g (9 oz) self-raising
   flour
1 teaspoon baking powder
pinch salt
75 g (3 oz) granulated
   sugar

1 teaspoon vanilla essence
2 eggs
75 g (3 oz) plain block
   chocolate
3 dl ($\frac{1}{2}$ pint) milk

Roughly chop the butter. Sift the flour with the baking powder and salt.

USE THE
METAL BLADE

Place the butter and the sugar in the Magimix bowl and process until the ingredients are light and creamy. Add the vanilla essence, scrape down the sides of the bowl and continue to process for 30 seconds. With the machine switched on, add the eggs, one by one through the feed tube processing after each addition until the ingredients are smooth and well mixed.

Melt the chocolate in a bowl over hot water and blend in the milk. Add the milk and chocolate to the mixture in the Magimix bowl and process until the ingredients are well mixed.

186

Add the flour mixture and switch on and off two or three times to mix the flour lightly into the other ingredients. Turn into a well greased 23 cm (9 in.) square cake tin (or bake in two layers) and bake in a moderate oven (180°C, 350°F, Reg. 4) for about 40 to 45 minutes until the cake is firm to the touch and a knitting needle plunged into the centre of the cake comes out clean. Leave to cool in the tin before turning out and filling or icing.

Rich chocolate filling for sponge cake

50 g (2 oz) plain block chocolate
50 g (2 oz) blanched almonds

50 g (2 oz) unsalted butter
50 g (2 oz) caster sugar

USE THE GRATING DISC

Grate the chocolate through the grating disc. Remove the chocolate.

USE THE METAL BLADE

Put the almonds in the Magimix bowl and process until the almonds are very finely ground. Add the butter and sugar to the almonds and process until the mixture is smooth, light and creamy. Add the grated chocolate and process for just long enough to mix the ingredients.

Butter filling

50 g (2 oz) butter

75 g (3 oz) icing sugar (see page 25)

USE THE METAL BLADE

Place the butter in the Magimix bowl and process until the butter is light and creamy. Add the icing sugar and process until the mixture is light and pale in colour.

FLAVOURING

1. *Chocolate*: dissolve 25 g (1 oz) plain block chocolate in a tablespoon water. Add the melted chocolate to the butter icing and process until the ingredients are well mixed. Or add 2 teaspoons cocoa powder and a few drops of vanilla essence into the butter icing and process until the ingredients are well mixed.

187

2. *Coffee*: add 2 teaspoons instant coffee to the butter icing and process until the ingredients are well mixed.

3. *Lemon*: add 2–3 teaspoons lemon juice to the butter icing and process until the ingredients are well mixed.

4. *Orange*: add 2–3 teaspoons orange juice to the butter icing and process until the ingredients are well mixed.

Almond paste icing for cakes

350 g (12 oz) blanched almonds
175 g (6 oz) icing sugar (see page 25)
juice of ¼ a lemon

¾ teaspoon orange flower water
¾ teaspoon vanilla essence
1–2 egg yolks

USE THE
METAL BLADE

Place the almonds in the Magimix bowl and process until the almonds are reduced to a paste. Add the icing sugar, lemon juice, orange flower water and vanilla essence and process until the ingredients are well mixed and smooth. With the machine on, add enough egg yolk for the mixture to form into a dry, pliable paste around the metal blade.

Note Brush the top and sides of a cake that is to be covered with almond paste with a glaze of apricot jam (thin 30 ml (2 tablespoons) apricot jam with 15 ml (1 tablespoon) of hot water) before applying the paste.

Roll out the almond paste as soon as possible after making and, having covered the cake with the almond paste, leave it to dry for 2 or 3 days before covering with royal icing.

Fruit and nut biscuits

25 g (1 oz) flour
pinch salt
½ teaspoon ground ginger
62 g (2½ oz) caster sugar

25 g (1 oz) golden syrup
25 g (1 oz) butter
25 g (1 oz) flaked almonds
25 g (1 oz) candied peel

USE THE
PLASTIC BLADE

Place the flour, salt and ginger in the Magimix bowl.

Combine the sugar, golden syrup and butter in a small saucepan and heat over a low flame until the sugar has melted and pour into the Magimix bowl. Process until the

188

ingredients are well mixed. Stop the machine, add the almonds and candied peel and process again until well mixed.

Drop teaspoons of the mixture on to oiled baking trays leaving plenty of space between each spoonful. Bake in a moderate oven (180°C, 350°F, Reg. 4) for 10–15 minutes until the biscuits are golden brown.

Leave the biscuits to cool slightly and, while they are still warm, remove them from the tray and cool completely on wire racks.

Flapjacks

100 g (4 oz) butter or margarine
62 g (2½ oz) sugar

1 tablespoon golden syrup
150 g (5 oz) rolled oats (or porridge oats)

Heat the butter, sugar and syrup in a small saucepan over a low heat until the sugar has melted.

USE THE
PLASTIC BLADE

Put the oats in the Magimix bowl and add the butter mixture. Process until the ingredients are well mixed. Spread the mixture in a greased baking pan about 18 × 33 cm (7 × 13 in.) and bake in a moderate oven (180°C, 350°F, Reg. 4) for 25–30 minutes until golden brown.

Cut into fingers while still warm and cool in the tin before turning out.

Teatime scones

350 g (¾ lb) plain flour
50 g (2 oz) lard
3 level teaspoons baking powder

¼ teaspoon salt
37 g (1½ oz) sugar
37 g (1½ oz) mixed peel
2.1 dl (7 fl. oz) milk

Preheat oven to 220°C, 425°F, Reg. 7.

USE THE
PLASTIC
BLADE

Combine the flour, lard (roughly chopped), baking powder and salt in the Magimix bowl and process until the mixture resembles fine breadcrumbs. Add the sugar and mixed peel and process until well mixed. With the machine

189

running, pour in all the milk at once through the feed tube and process until the dough forms a ball around the blade.

Roll out the dough on a well floured board at about 2 cm ($\frac{3}{4}$ in.) thick and cut out the scones with a 5 cm (2 in.) cutter. Place the scones on a greased baking sheet and brush with a little milk. Bake in a hot oven (220°C, 425°F, Reg. 7) for 10–15 minutes until the scones are golden brown.

Remove the scones from the baking sheet and leave to cool slightly on wire racks before serving.

Almond biscuits

100 g (4 oz) butter or
    margarine
100 g (4 oz) sugar
1 egg yolk
$\frac{1}{2}$ teaspoon almond essence

175 g (6 oz) plain flour
1 teaspoon baking powder
pinch salt
approx. 18 blanched
    almonds

Split each almond in half and set aside.

USE THE
METAL BLADE

Roughly chop the butter and combine it with the sugar in the Magimix bowl. Process, scraping down the sides of the bowl occasionally, until the mixture is smooth, pale and creamy. With the machine running, add the egg yolk and almond essence through the feed tube.

Turn the machine off and add the flour, baking powder and salt to the ingredients in the bowl. Process until the ingredients are well mixed. Roll the mixture into small balls and place on greased baking sheets leaving a small space between the balls. Place a split almond on each ball and press in firmly.

Bake in a moderate oven (180°C, 350°F, Reg. 4) for 20–25 minutes until the biscuits are a pale golden colour. Remove from the sheets and cool on a wire rack.

Coconut shortbread

100 g (4 oz) butter
50 g (2 oz) sugar
50 g (2 oz) desiccated
coconut

pinch of salt
150 g (5 oz) plain flour

USE THE
METAL BLADE Roughly chop the butter and combine with the sugar in
the Magimix bowl. Process, scraping down the sides of the
bowl, until the mixture is smooth, pale and creamy. Add
the coconut, salt and flour and process until the mixture
forms a ball around the blade. If it seems too dry add a
little more butter.

Roll the mixture out on a lightly floured board to about
2 cm ($\frac{3}{4}$ in.) thick and cut into fingers. Place on greased
baking trays and mark the tops of the fingers with the
prongs of a fork. Bake in a moderate oven (180°C, 350°F,
Reg. 4) for 20–25 minutes until the shortbread is a pale
golden colour. Remove the biscuits from the tray and cool
on a wire rack.

Banana brandysnaps

3 bananas
1 teaspoon lemon juice

60 ml (2 fl. oz) double
cream
100 g ($\frac{1}{4}$ lb) brandysnaps

USE THE
METAL BLADE Peel the bananas and cut them into quarters. Sprinkle
them with the lemon juice to prevent browning. Place the
bananas and cream in the Magimix bowl and process until
smooth. Fill the brandysnaps with the banana cream and
serve.

Butter wafers

Light slim biscuits that go equally well with ice cream or
with a cup of tea.

100 g (4 oz) butter
75 g (3 oz) sugar
1 egg
few drops vanilla essence

grated rind of $\frac{1}{2}$ a lemon
75 g (3 oz) self-raising
flour

191

Place the butter and sugar in the Magimix bowl and process until light and creamy. Add the egg, a few drops of vanilla essence and the lemon rind and process until the ingredients are well mixed. Add the flour and process until the ingredients are well mixed.

Drop the mixture from a teaspoon, allowing a generous space between each teaspoonful, onto a greased baking sheet. Bake in a moderately hot oven (190°C, 375°F, Reg. 5) for about 10 minutes or until the wafers have spread and are just turning golden brown around the edges – take care not to overcook and burn.

Chocolate drop cookies

One of the most delicious of all home-made biscuits – quick to make, quick to cook and mouth-melting to eat. Makes about 36 biscuits.

*50 g (2 oz) plain slab
    chocolate
50 g (2 oz) almonds
100 g (4 oz) brown sugar
100 g (4 oz) granulated
    sugar
100 g (4 oz) butter*

*1 egg
few drops vanilla essence
275 g (10 oz) self-raising
    flour
25 g (1 oz) mixed dried
    fruit*

Break up the chocolate.

Place the chocolate and almonds in the Magimix bowl and process until the chocolate is chopped to the size of small peas. Remove the chocolate and almonds.

Place the sugars and butter in the Magimix bowl and process until the mixture is well mixed. Add the egg and and vanilla essence and continue to process until the mixture forms a smooth dough. Add the flour, chocolate, almonds and mixed dried fruit and switch on and off three or four times to mix the ingredients.

Drop the mixture from a teaspoon, leaving generous spaces between each biscuit, onto a well greased baking sheet. Bake in a moderately hot oven (190°C, 375°F, Reg. 5) for 10–15 minutes until golden brown. Slide off the hot baking sheet onto wire racks and leave to cool.

Fairling biscuits

100 g (4 oz) flour
pinch salt
$\frac{1}{4}$ teaspoon of ground
  ginger, mixed spice and
  ground cinnamon

$1\frac{1}{2}$ teaspoons bicarbonate
  of soda
50 g (2 oz) butter
50 g (2 oz) sugar
2 tablespoons golden syrup

USE THE
METAL BLADE

Combine the flour, salt, ginger, mixed spice, cinnamon and bicarbonate of soda in the Magimix bowl and process until well mixed. Roughly chop the butter and add it to the ingredients in the Magimix bowl. Process until the mixture is reduced to the consistency of fine breadcrumbs. With the machine running, add the sugar through the feed tube.

Melt the golden syrup in a small saucepan. With the machine running, pour the syrup onto the other ingredients through the feed tube and process until the mixture is smooth.

Drop the mixture from a teaspoon 5 cm (2 in.) apart onto a greased baking sheet. Bake the biscuits in a moderate oven (180°C, 350°F, Reg. 4) for 10 minutes. Remove the tray from the oven, tap it on a hard surface to spread the biscuits and return to the oven for a further 5 minutes or until the biscuits are firm.

Ginger biscuits

175 g (6 oz) plain flour
pinch salt
1 teaspoon bicarbonate
  soda
2 teaspoons ground ginger

50 g (2 oz) sugar
50 g (2 oz) lard
$1\frac{1}{2}$ tablespoons golden
  syrup
1 egg

USE THE
PLASTIC BLADE

Combine the flour, salt, bicarbonate of soda, ginger and sugar in the Magimix bowl and process until the ingredients are well mixed.

Combine the lard and golden syrup in a saucepan and heat until the lard has melted. Leave to cool for 2 minutes. With the motor running, add the golden syrup and lard through the feed tube processing until the ingredients are well mixed. Add the egg through the feed tube and process until the mixture is smooth.

193

Roll the mixture into walnut sized balls and place them, well spread out, on a greased baking sheet. Bake in a moderately hot oven (190°C, 375°F, Reg. 5) for about 20 minutes until firm. Leave to set, slide off the baking sheet and cool on a wire rack.

Basic white bread

Enough for 1 small loaf.

6 g ($\frac{1}{4}$ oz) fresh yeast (or 1 teaspoon dried yeast)
1.5 dl ($\frac{1}{4}$ pint) warm water
$\frac{1}{2}$ teaspoon sugar

225 g (8 oz) strong plain flour
1 teaspoon salt
6 g ($\frac{1}{4}$ oz) lard

Mix fresh yeast to a paste with the sugar and blend in the warm water (or combine warm water with the sugar, mix until the sugar is dissolved and whisk in the dried yeast). Leave to stand for 10 minutes in a warm place until spongy. Cut the lard into small pieces.

USE THE
METAL BLADE

Combine the flour, salt and lard in the Magimix bowl and process for a short time to cut the lard into the flour. With the machine switched on, add the yeast liquid through the feed tube, process for long enough for the dough to form a ball around the metal blade and then process for a further 20 seconds. Remove the dough, dust with flour, place in a lightly oiled polythene bag, leaving enough space for rising, and leave to rise in a warm place for about 1 hour or until doubled in bulk.

Remove the dough from the bag, knock down with the knuckles of both hands to knock out the air bubbles and return dough to the Magimix. Process for 10 seconds to knead the dough and remove from the bowl. Shape into an oblong, fold in three and place in a well greased loaf tin with the seam underneath. Place the tin back in the oiled polythene bag and leave to rise in a warm place for 40 minutes.

Brush the top of the loaf with 1 tablespoon salt dissolved in 3 tablespoons water and bake in a very hot oven (230°C, 450°F, Reg. 8) for 30 minutes covering the top of the loaf with a sheet of greaseproof paper if it gets too brown.

Turn out on a wire rack and leave to cool.

Brioches

1 tablespoon caster sugar
1½ tablespoons warm water
2 teaspoons dried yeast
50 g (2 oz) butter

3 eggs
225 g (8 oz) plain flour
¼ teaspoon salt

Dissolve ½ teaspoon sugar in the warm water, sprinkle the dried yeast on top, whisk lightly and leave until spongy (about 10 minutes). Melt the butter and leave to cool.

USE THE
METAL BLADE

Place 2 eggs in the Magimix bowl and process until smooth. Add the flour, salt, remaining sugar and melted butter. Switch on the machine and pour the yeast mixture in through the feed tube, processing for long enough for the dough to form a ball around the knife. Continue to process for 1 minute, turn the dough onto a floured board and knead lightly with the fingertips for 1 minute. Place it in a lightly oiled polythene bag and leave to rise in a warm place for 2 hours or until doubled in bulk.

Grease twelve brioche or castle pudding tins. Turn the risen dough onto a floured board and divide into twelve pieces. Knead each piece lightly and form three-quarters of it into a ball. Place the balls in the tins and press a finger firmly into the centre. Roll the remaining dough into twelve small balls and place them on top of the dough in the tins. Place the tins in an oiled polythene bag and leave to rise in a warm place for 1 hour until well risen.

Place the remaining egg in the Magimix bowl and add a teaspoon water. Process until smooth. Brush the risen brioches with the egg glaze and bake them in a very hot oven (230°C, 450°F, Reg. 8) for 10 minutes or until golden brown. Serve the brioches as soon as possible.

Note This dough can also be used to make a covering for a skinned savoury sausage or for a pâté. After the first rise, roll the dough out into an oblong. Fill with the chosen filling. Roll up neatly and leave to rise for 40 minutes in a warm place. Brush with an egg glaze and then bake in a hot oven until well risen and golden brown. Serve cut into slices.

195

Making batters for pancakes, fritters and Yorkshire puddings with your Magimix food processor

Batters, pancake mixes and fritter mixtures need to be absolutely smooth if the best results are to be obtained. With your Magimix food processor all the hard work of mixing the flour with the other ingredients is done for you and the resulting batters will be as light as they could be. Most batters can be used straight from the Magimix food processor without being left to stand for some time before cooking.

Different ingredients need different batters; fritters, for instance, need a light batter (an egg white, stiffly beaten, can be added for extra lightness), whereas something like fish fillets which are to be deep fried in batter need to have a firmer mixture that will adhere to the fish while it is cooking.

Follow one of the recipes in this book or use your own favourite mixture, combine all the ingredients in the Magimix bowl, using the metal blade, and process until the batter is smooth.

Basic pancake batter

Makes about 8 pancakes.

100g (4 oz) plain flour
2 eggs
3 dl (½ pint) milk

¼ teaspoon salt
50 g (2 oz) butter, melted
oil for frying

Combine the flour, eggs, milk, salt and cooled melted butter in the Magimix bowl. Switch on and process until the mixture is smooth, scraping down the sides of the bowl if necessary. Pour into a jug and leave to stand for 10 minutes before using.

Heat a very thin film of oil or lard in an omelette pan until smoking, add a small amount of batter and swirl it around the pan until it forms a thin skin across the bottom. Cook over a medium high heat until golden brown underneath, turn over and cook until golden brown on the other side. Slide the pancake on to a warm plate and continue with the rest of the batter, stacking the pancakes and keeping them warm as each one is made.

196

Fritter batter I for sliced vegetables

This is a good batter for thinly sliced vegetables such as aubergines, courgettes or courgette flowers.

Dip the slices of vegetables or flowers in the batter and deep fry them for 5 minutes in very deep hot oil. Drain them well and serve with a tomato sauce (see page 158).

$2\frac{1}{2}$ tablespoons flour
1 egg
1 tablespoon olive oil

3 tablespoons water
salt and white pepper

USE THE
METAL BLADE

Combine all the ingredients in the Magimix food processor and season with salt and pepper. Process until the batter is smooth.

Fritter batter II for vegetables

A very light crisp batter which goes well with thin slices of fennel and cauliflower sprigs etc.

$1\frac{1}{2}$ tablespoons flour
1.5 dl ($\frac{1}{4}$ pint) water

salt and white pepper
1 egg white

USE THE
METAL BLADE

Place the flour in the Magimix bowl with the water. Season with salt and pepper and process until the batter is smooth. Beat the egg white in a bowl until stiff. Lightly fold in the batter, mixing for only just long enough to mix in the batter. Use the batter at once.

Pancakes stuffed with ham and mushrooms

Serves 6

6–8 pancakes (see opposite
   page)
4 sprigs parsley
50 g (2 oz) Cheddar cheese
175 g (6 oz) firm button
   mushrooms

50 g (2 oz) butter
salt and freshly ground
   black pepper
6–8 thin slices lean ham

USE THE
METAL BLADE

Remove the tough stalks from the parsley. Place the parsley leaves in the Magimix bowl and process until the leaves are finely chopped. Remove the parsley.

197

Grate the cheese through the grating disc. Remove the cheese.

Slice the mushrooms through the slicing disc.

Melt half the butter in a frying pan. Add the mushrooms and cook over a low heat for about 3 minutes until the butter has been absorbed into the mushrooms. Add the parsley, season with salt and pepper and mix lightly. Lay a slice of ham on each pancake and spread over the mushroom mixture. Roll the pancakes up neatly and arrange them in a lightly greased baking dish. Sprinkle over the cheese and pour over the remaining butter, melted.

Bake the pancakes in a hot oven (200°C, 400°F, Reg. 6) for 10 minutes until they are hot through and golden brown on the top.

Spinach stuffed pancakes

Serves 6

6–8 pancakes (see page 196)
450 g (1 lb) fresh or frozen spinach
1 small onion
4 tomatoes
25 g (1 oz) Parmesan cheese

50 g (2 oz) butter
salt and freshly ground black pepper
pinch paprika
4 hard-boiled eggs

Cook the spinach in a little boiling, salted water until just tender. Drain well, place in a colander and press with the fingers to remove as much moisture as possible. Peel and roughly chop the onion. Cover the tomatoes with boiling water for about 1 minute then drain well and slide off the skins. Roughly chop the tomatoes.

Place the Parmesan cheese in the Magimix bowl and process until the cheese is very finely ground. Remove the cheese. Place the onion in the Magimix bowl and process until the onion is finely chopped. Remove the onion. Place the tomatoes in the Magimix bowl and process until the tomatoes are reduced to a purée.

Melt 1 oz butter in a frying pan, add the onion and cook over a low heat until the onion is soft and transparent.

Add the tomatoes, season with salt, freshly ground black pepper and a pinch of paprika pepper, mix well and cook over a low heat for 10 minutes.

USE THE
SLICING DISC Slice the hard-boiled eggs through the slicing disc. Add the eggs to the tomato mixture and mix lightly.

Spread each pancake with some of the spinach topped with some of the tomato mixture and roll up neatly. Place the pancakes in a lightly greased baking dish, sprinkle over the Parmesan cheese and pour over the remaining butter melted and bake in a hot oven (200°C, 400°F, Reg. 6) for 10 minutes until the pancakes are hot through and the top is golden brown.

Pancakes filled with Brie

A delicious combination but a little on the rich side so it should only be followed by a light main course.

Serves 6

pancake batter (see page 196)
50 g (2 oz) Parmesan cheese
6 g ($\frac{1}{4}$ oz) butter

2 teaspoons flour
6 tablespoons milk
100 g (4 oz) ripe Brie
salt and freshly ground black pepper

Follow the recipe for making pancakes on page 196.
Break up the Parmesan.

USE THE
METAL BLADE Put the Parmesan cheese into the Magimix bowl and process until the cheese is reduced to a powder. Remove the Parmesan.

Melt the butter in a saucepan. Add the flour and mix well. Gradually add the milk, stirring continually over a medium high heat until the sauce is thick and smooth. Put the sauce in the Magimix bowl with the Brie, season with salt and pepper and process until the ingredients are reduced to a smooth paste.

Spread the pancakes with a thin layer of the cheese mixture and roll each one up neatly. Arrange the rolled pancakes in a lightly greased fireproof serving dish, sprinkle over the Parmesan and bake in a moderately hot oven (190°C, 375°F, Reg. 5) for 15–20 minutes until the pancakes are hot through and the Parmesan has melted and is golden brown.

199

Boxty

Crisp pancakes made with a combination of batter and grated potatoes.

Serves 4–6

450 (1 lb) potatoes (the floury kind are best)
50 g (2 oz) plain flour
½ teaspoon salt

3 tablespoons milk
freshly ground black pepper
50 g (2 oz) butter or clarified bacon fat

Peel and roughly chop the potatoes. Cover them with cold water to prevent discolouration.

USE THE
METAL BLADE

Combine the flour, salt and milk in the Magimix bowl and season with freshly ground black pepper. Process until the mixture becomes a smooth batter. Turn the batter into a bowl.

USE THE
GRATING DISC

Grate the potatoes through the grating disc and turn them into the batter. Mix well.

Melt the butter in a heavy pan until foaming. Add table-spoons of the batter and cook over a moderate heat for about 3 minutes on each side until crisp and golden brown. Drain the cakes on kitchen paper and keep warm while frying the rest.

Traditionally Boxty is served with crisply fried or grilled bacon but the potato cakes go extremely well with many main course dishes.

Puddings

Old fashioned custard pie

175 g (6 oz) pâté sablée
  (see page 179)
1 egg
2 egg yolks
25 g (1 oz) sugar
12 g (½ oz) flour

1.5 dl (¼ pint) milk
1.5 dl (¼ pint) single
  cream
12 g (½ oz) melted butter
½ teaspoon grated nutmeg

USE THE
PLASTIC BLADE

Combine the egg, egg yolks, sugar and flour in the Magimix food processor and process until well mixed. With the machine running, add the milk through the feed tube. Stop the machine and add the cream, melted butter and ground nutmeg. Process for just long enough to mix the ingredients.

Roll out the pastry thinly on a floured board and line a 18–20 cm (7–8 in.) well greased flan tin with the pastry. Pour the custard into the pastry case and bake the pie in a hot oven (200°C, 400°F, Reg. 6) for 30–35 minutes until set. The pie should be a light golden brown; if it begins to brown too quickly, cover it with a sheet of buttered greaseproof paper.

Leave to cool for 10 minutes and serve warm or cold with cream.

Tarte aux amandes

Serves 6–8

pâté sablée (see page 179)
5 tablespoons apricot jam
100 g (4 oz) blanched
* almonds*
2 eggs, separated

225 g (8 oz) caster sugar
¼ teaspoon vanilla essence
3 tablespoons milk
pinch salt
2 tablespoons icing sugar

Roll out the pastry and line a 20 cm (8 in.) flan tin. Chill the case, spread it with the apricot jam and bake in the centre of a moderately hot oven (190°C, 375°F, Reg. 5) for 10 minutes. Prick the bottom of the case with a fork if it has risen during the cooking time.

USE THE
METAL BLADE

Place the almonds in the Magimix bowl and process until they are reduced to a fine powder. Remove the almonds. Place the egg yolks and the sugar in the Magimix bowl and process until the mixture is smooth, pale yellow, light and fluffy. Add the almonds, vanilla, milk and a pinch of salt and continue to process until the ingredients are well mixed.

Beat the egg whites until stiff and lightly fold in the egg yolk mixture. Pour the filling into the pastry case and return the flan to the bottom of the oven and cook for a further 15 minutes until the filling has risen and is golden brown. Sprinkle over the icing sugar and bake for a further 5 minutes until the sugar has melted.

Steamed apple pudding

Serves 4

200 g (7 oz) self-raising
* flour*
pinch salt
87 g (3½ oz) shredded suet
cold water
450 g (1 lb) cooking apples

1 tablespoon sultanas
100 g (4 oz) caster sugar
pinch cinnamon
pinch nutmeg
grated rind of half a lemon

USE THE
PLASTIC BLADE

Place the flour, salt and shredded suet in the Magimix bowl. Add a little cold water and turn the machine on. Process until the mixture has formed a ball around the blade, adding a little more water through the feed tube if necessary. Remove the dough.

Peel and quarter the apples.

Slice the apples through the slicing disc. Remove the apples.

Reserve one-third of the pastry and roll the remainder out on a floured board. Line a well greased pudding basin with the pastry. Combine the sultanas, sugar, spices and lemon rind. Arrange layers of the apples in the basin sprinkling the layers with the sugar mixture.

Roll out the remaining pastry, place on top of the pudding, damp the edges and press firmly together. Cover tightly with buttered foil and stand in a saucepan filled two-thirds of the way up the basin with boiling water. Steam for $2\frac{1}{2}$ hours or for 50 minutes in a pressure cooker.

Alexander pudding

Serves 4

*175 g (6 oz) white bread
  with the crusts removed
100 g (4 oz) sugar
100 g (4 oz) butter*

*3 eggs
grated rind and juice of 1
  large lemon
1 tablespoon marmalade*

Process the bread until reduced to coarse breadcrumbs. Remove the bread. Combine the sugar and butter (roughly chopped) in the Magimix bowl and process until the mixture is white and creamy. Separate the eggs and add the yolks, one at a time, to the mixture in the Magimix bowl through the feed tube with the motor running. Stop the machine, add the breadcrumbs, rind and juice of the lemon and 1 tablespoon marmalade and process until ingredients are well mixed.

Beat the egg whites in a large bowl until very stiff. Lightly fold the mixture from the Magimix bowl into the egg whites. Butter a pudding basin and pour in the mixture, cover with buttered greaseproof paper or foil and steam for about $1\frac{1}{4}$ hours or until a skewer plunged into the centre of the pudding comes out clean.

203

Lemon pudding

Serves 4–6

200 g (7 oz) self-raising flour
87 g (3½ oz) shredded suet
cold water to mix

150 g (5 oz) brown sugar
75 g (3 oz) butter
1 lemon

USE THE
METAL BLADE Place the flour, shredded suet and a little cold water in the Magimix food processor. Process for a few seconds and with the machine still running add a little more water through the feed tube allowing time for the ingredients to mix until the dough forms a ball around the blade. Remove the dough from the bowl.

Reserving one-third of the dough, roll out the remainder on a floured board and line a buttered pudding basin with it. Place one-third of the sugar and butter in the bottom of the basin. Quarter the lemon and place it in the basin. Cover with the remaining butter and sugar. Roll out the remaining dough to form a lid, damping the edges and joining together firmly. Cover the basin tightly with buttered foil and steam for 2½ hours.

Indian carrot pudding

Serves 6

Carrot puddings always sound rather strange but in fact many variations of these sweet puddings were very popular in Britain during the last century. Sugar brings out the natural sweetness of the root vegetables resulting in a pudding that is very popular with children.

900 g (2 lb) carrots
25 g (1 oz) pistachio nuts (blanched)
25 g (1 oz) almonds (blanched)

9 dl (1½ pints) milk
50 g (2 oz) melted butter
100 g (4 oz) caster sugar

USE THE
METAL BLADE Combine the nuts in the Magimix bowl and process until finely chopped. Remove the nuts.

USE THE
SHREDDING DISC Peel the carrots and shred them through the shredding disc. Combine the carrots and milk in a saucepan and cook over a low heat until the carrots are soft and the milk has been absorbed. Add the butter and sugar and continue to cook, stirring all the time, for 5 minutes. Mix in the nuts and serve very hot with cream.

Swiss apple charlotte

900 g (2 lb) cooking apples
100 g (4 oz) sugar
2 tablespoons sweet white wine
grated rind of $\frac{1}{2}$ a lemon

1 long French roll
melted butter
3 tablespoons strawberry jam

USE THE
METAL BLADE

Peel, core and roughly chop the apples. Combine the apples with the sugar and wine in a saucepan and cook over a low heat, stirring every now and then to prevent sticking, until the apples are soft. Add the lemon rind, place the mixture in the Magimix bowl and process until the apples are well puréed.

Cut the bread into 6 mm ($\frac{1}{4}$ in.) thick slices. Dip the slices in melted butter and use them to line the bottom and sides of a lightly greased baking dish. Spoon in the apple, dot with spoonsful of jam and cover with a final layer of bread.

Bake the pudding in a hot oven (200°C, 400°F, Reg. 6) until the top is crisp and golden brown, about 25–30 minutes.

Serve hot with cream.

Apple custard

Serves 6

Much more superior than a straightforward apple snow or fluff and, with the Magimix food processor, just as quick to make. You can serve the pudding hot or cold or use it as a base for other puddings that include custard in the recipe.

675 g ($1\frac{1}{2}$ lb) cooking apples
$\frac{1}{4}$ teaspoon ground coriander
$\frac{1}{4}$ teaspoon cinnamon
pinch ground cloves

100 g (4 oz) sugar
juice and grated rind of 1 lemon
3 medium eggs
1.5 dl ($\frac{1}{4}$ pint) double cream

Peel, core and roughly chop the apples. Combine the apples in a saucepan with the spices, sugar, lemon juice and rind. Bring to the boil and simmer until the apples are soft.

205

Place the eggs in the Magimix bowl and process until the eggs are well beaten and light. With the machine switched on, add the stewed apples, a spoonful at a time until the bowl is full. Process until smooth and turn into a bowl. Place the remaining apple in the Magimix bowl and process until smooth. With the machine switched on, add the cream through the feed tube, pouring it in a steady stream.

Add the apple and cream mixture to the apple custard and mix well. Turn the mixture into a large, heavy saucepan and cook over a very low heat, stirring continually, until the custard thickens (this will take about 5 minutes).

Pour into a bowl and serve at once or leave to cool and then refrigerate.

Délice de pommes

Serves 6–8

A real nectar of a pudding and one that you can serve equally well for a hearty farmhouse lunch or a smart dinner party. The pudding can be eaten hot or cold.

*50 g (2 oz) blanched
  almonds
900 g (2 lb) cooking apples
3 dl (½ pint) water
225 g (8 oz) sugar
grated rind and juice of 1
  lemon*

*pinch ground cloves
pinch ground cinnamon
2 eggs
100 g (4 oz) flour
1.5 dl (¼ pint) double
  cream
few drops vanilla essence*

Slice the almonds through the slicing disc and remove them from the bowl. Peel and core the apples and slice them through the slicing disc.

Combine the water and 100 g (4 oz) sugar in a saucepan with the lemon juice, lemon rind, cloves and cinnamon. Bring to the boil and stir until the sugar is dissolved. Add the sliced apples and simmer very slowly for 20 minutes or until the apple slices are transparent.

Combine the eggs and remaining sugar in the Magimix bowl and process until the mixture is smooth and pale yellow. Add the flour and process until well mixed. With the machine running, add the cream through the feed tube and process for 20 seconds. Add the almonds and vanilla and process until the ingredients are well mixed – do not over-process or the almonds will become too finely chopped. Turn the cooked apples into a baking dish and pour over the topping in a thin layer.

Bake the pudding in a moderate oven (180°C, 350°F, Reg. 4) for 45 minutes until the topping is set and a delicious, crisp, golden brown.

Iced nut cake

Serves 6–8

A really rich and mouth-watering sweet which can be made well in advance.

100 g (4 oz) softened, unsalted butter
100 g (4 oz) caster sugar
1 large egg, separated
25 g (1 oz) shelled, blanched almonds
25 g (1 oz) shelled walnuts
2 tablespoons Kirsch
1 tablespoon water
24 sponge fingers
1.5 dl ($\frac{1}{4}$ pint) cream
8 walnut halves

USE THE
METAL BLADE
Combine the butter and sugar in the Magimix bowl and process until the mixture is light and fluffy. Add the egg yolk and process until smooth. Add the blanched almonds and walnuts and process until nuts are finely chopped. Whip the egg white in a bowl until stiff and lightly fold in the nut mixture.

Combine the Kirsch and water. Line a loaf tin with foil. Cover the bottom with sponge fingers and sprinkle the fingers with the Kirsch and water mixture. Cover with a layer of the nut mixture and then with more sponge fingers. Continue with the layers ending with one of sponge fingers and sprinkling each layer of fingers with the Kirsch mixture. Cover with foil and refrigerate for at least 5 hours. Turn out onto a serving dish and remove the foil.

Whip the cream until stiff and mask the cake with the cream. Garnish with the halved walnuts and serve well chilled.

Fruit sorbets and water ices

Serves 4–6

Delicious summer desserts can be made by combining fruit juice or purée with a sugar syrup and egg whites. Beating the mixture after it has been half frozen is an essential step in making these ices and this can be done quickly and efficiently in your Magimix.

3 dl (½ pint) water | juice 1½ lemons
175 g (6 oz) sugar | 2 egg whites
3 dl (½ pint) fresh orange
  juice

Combine the water and sugar in a saucepan, bring to the boil and boil over a high heat for 5 minutes. Leave to cool. Combine the syrup and fruit juice and pour into shallow freezing trays. Freeze in the freezing compartment of the refrigerator or in the deep freeze until the mixture has crystallized but is not completely solid.

Whip the egg whites until stiff.

USE THE
METAL BLADE

Break up the half-frozen ice and turn it into the Magimix bowl. Process until the mixture is just smooth. Add the egg whites and process for just long enough to mix the ingredients. Return the ice to the freezing trays and continue to freeze until it is solid.

Variations

Purée strawberries, raspberries, cooked red or black currants or rhubarb in the Magimix using the metal blade. Measure 3 dl (½ pint) of purée, add the juice of 1 lemon and continue in the same way as above.

Yoghurt ice cream

Serves 4

Less expensive than a cream ice cream as well as being far less fattening and extremely easy to make. The texture of yoghurt responds ideally to ice cream and the range of flavours you can produce is amazing.

2 eggs, separated | 1.5 dl (¼ pint) plain
100–175 g (4–6 oz) sugar | yoghurt
1.5 (¼ pint) water and
  juice of ½ a lemon (or
  use fruit juice)

Place the egg yolks and sugar in the Magimix bowl and process until pale yellow in colour and until the mixture is light and fluffy. Heat the water and lemon juice or fruit juice until boiling. With the machine running, pour the boiling liquid through the feed tube onto the egg yolks and sugar and process until well mixed. Add the yoghurt and process until the mixture is well blended.

Turn into a freezing tray and freeze in the ice making compartment of a refrigerator or in a deep freeze until the mixture is just firm to the touch (about 1 hour). Break up the ice cream and return it to the Magimix bowl. Process until smooth and creamy.

Beat the egg whites until stiff, lightly fold in the creamed mixture and return to the freezing tray. Freeze until solid.

Remove the ice cream from the freezer for 10 minutes before spooning out.

Variations

Passion fruit ice cream

Strain the juice from a large tin of passion fruit pulp. Heat the pulp until boiling, add it to the egg yolks and sugar and continue as for the basic recipe.

Redcurrant, blackcurrant or raspberry ice cream

Cook 350 g (12 oz) redcurrants, blackcurrants or raspberries with 90 ml (3 fl. oz) water and enough sugar to sweeten until the fruit is tender. Rub the fruit through a sieve.

Process the egg yolks in the Magimix bowl until they are smooth and light. Heat the fruit purée to boiling point and, with the machine running, pour it onto the egg yolks through the feed tube. Process until the ingredients are well mixed and light. Proceed in the same way as for the basic recipe.

Strawberry ice cream

Purée 225–350 g (8–12 oz) strawberries. Heat the purée and thin it with a little water or orange juice. Proceed in exactly the same way as for the basic recipe, pouring the hot purée onto the egg yolks and sugar through the feed tube.

Banana ice cream

1.5 dl ($\frac{1}{4}$ pint) water　　　　3 bananas
juice of 1 lemon

Combine the water and lemon juice and heat until boiling. Process the egg yolks with the sugar as in the basic recipe. Add the boiling liquid, pouring it through the feed tube with the motor running. Add the bananas, roughly broken up, and process until the mixture is smooth. Add the yoghurt and continue in exactly the same way as for the basic recipe.

Passion fruit fool

Serves 4

The pips provide a crunchy contrast to the smoothness of this sweet so do not remove them.

12 passion fruit　　　　3 dl ($\frac{1}{2}$ pint) double cream
75 g (3 oz) sugar

Scoop out the fruit from the shells. Combine the fruit pulp with the sugar and leave to stand for 15 minutes.

USE THE
PLASTIC BLADE

Place the cream in the Magimix bowl and process until it just begins to thicken. Add the passion fruit pulp and process for just long enough to mix the ingredients. Spoon into four goblets and chill for at least 1 hour before serving.

Rum and raisin ice cream (using cream)

Serves 4–6

100 g (4 oz) raisins or
   mixed dried fruit
3 tablespoons rum
4 egg yolks

3 dl ($\frac{1}{2}$ pint) milk
175 g (6 oz) caster sugar
$\frac{1}{2}$ teaspoon vanilla essence
3 dl ($\frac{1}{2}$ pint) double cream

USE THE
METAL BLADE

Soak the raisins in the rum while making the custard. Put the egg yolks in the Magimix bowl and process until the egg yolks are smooth but not frothy.

Combine the milk and sugar with the vanilla essence in a saucepan and bring to boiling point. Remove the pan from the heat, switch on the Magimix and slowly pour the milk onto the egg yolks through the feed tube with the machine in action. Switch off as soon as the milk has been added.

Transfer the mixture to a double saucepan and place over a pan of hot, but not boiling, water. Stir over a medium heat until the custard thickens enough to coat the back of a wooden spoon. Remove from the heat, add the raisins and rum and continue to stir until the mixture cools to prevent a skin forming. Leave until the mixture is cold.

Whip the cream until thick with a rotary whisk and fold it lightly into the custard base. Spoon the custard into a metal container (I use a cake tin) and put it into the freezing compartment of a refrigerator or into a deep freeze.

When the ice cream has frozen to a depth of about 1 cm ($\frac{1}{2}$ in.) around the edges of the container remove it from the refrigerator or freezer and scoop it out into the Magimix bowl. Process with the metal blade until the ice cream is smooth and light, turn immediately back into the metal container and wrap it in foil. Return to the freezer for a further 2 hours or until solid.

Serve in scoops in glass globlets and top, if you like, with a chocolate sauce or hot syrup sauce.

Basic custard ice cream

Serves 4–6

4 eggs
100 g (4 oz) granulated
 sugar
4.5 dl (¾ pint) milk

¼ teaspoon vanilla essence
flavouring (see 'Flavouring
 variations')

USE THE
METAL BLADE

Combine the eggs, sugar and vanilla essence in the Magi-mix bowl and process until the mixture is light and pale yellow.

Bring the milk to boiling point in a saucepan.

With the motor running, pour the milk through the feed tube onto the eggs and process for just long enough to mix the ingredients – do not over-process. Turn the custard into the top of a double boiler or into a thick, heavy pan and cook over hot but not boiling water, or over a very very low heat, stirring continually until the custard thickens and coats the back of a wooden spoon. Add the vanilla essence and continue to stir off the heat until the custard cools.

Add the flavouring.

Turn the mixture into freezing trays and freeze in a deep freeze or the freezing compartment of a refrigerator until the ice cream has frozen to a depth of about 2 cm ¾ in.) around the sides of the trays.

Turn the ice cream back into the Magimix bowl and process until smooth. Turn back into the freezing trays, packing down firmly, and freeze until firm.

Remove the ice cream from the freezer or refrigerator 10 minutes before serving.

Flavouring variations

Banana ice cream

basic ice cream custard   *3 bananas*

Make the custard as for basic custard ice cream recipe and leave to cool. Peel the bananas.

USE THE
METAL BLADE

Place the bananas in the Magimix bowl and process until the bananas are reduced to a smooth purée. Add the custard and process until the ingredients are well mixed. Turn into trays and freeze in the same way as the basic recipe.

Avocado ice cream

Serves 4–6

An unusual but delicious ice cream which is very good for small children as it is easy to digest. Fresh limes are fairly easy to find these days and the juice is really essential to this sweet.

basic ice cream custard
2 medium sized, ripe
* avocadoes*

30 g (2 oz) sugar
juice of $\frac{1}{2}$ a small lime

Make the custard as for the basic custard ice cream recipe and leave to cool. Peel the avocadoes and remove the stones.

USE THE
METAL BLADE

Combine the avocadoes, sugar and lime juice in the Magimix bowl and process until the ingredients are reduced to a smooth purée. Add the cooled custard and process until the mixture is smooth.

Turn into freezer trays and freeze in the same way as the basic recipe.

Rum and raisin ice cream

basic ice cream custard
100 g (4 oz) raisins

2 tablespoons dark rum

Make the custard as for the basic custard ice cream recipe and leave to cool.

USE THE
METAL BLADE

Combine the raisins and rum in the Magimix bowl and process until the raisins are coarsely chopped. Add the cooled custard and continue to process until the ingredients are well mixed.

Turn into freezer trays and freeze as for the basic recipe.

Mango ice cream

You can find mangoes fairly easily these days but they are inclined to be a little on the unripe side. Put unripe mangoes in a brown paper bag and leave them in a sunny or warm place until they are well coloured and soft.

2 mangoes   *basic custard ice cream*
2 teaspoons lemon or lime
* juice*

Make the custard as for the basic ice cream custard recipe and leave to cool.

USE THE
METAL BLADE

Peel the mangoes and remove the stones. Combine the mangoes and lemon or lime juice in the Magimix bowl and process until the fruit is reduced to a smooth purée.

Add the custard and continue to process until the ingredients are smooth.

Turn into freezing trays and freeze in the same way as for the basic recipe.

Chocolate ice cream

Serves 6

2 eggs   *3 dl ($\frac{1}{2}$ pint) milk*
2 egg yolks   *few drops vanilla essence*
50 g (2 oz) caster sugar *3 dl ($\frac{1}{2}$ pint) double cream*
200 g (7 oz) plain
* chocolate*

USE THE
PLASTIC BLADE

Combine the eggs, egg yolks and sugar in the Magimix bowl. Process until mixed.

Break the chocolate into pieces and put them in a saucepan with the milk. Stir over a low heat until the chocolate has completely dissolved and the milk is hot but not boiling. With the Magimix food processor in action pour the chocolate milk onto the egg mixture through the feed tube and process until the ingredients are amalgamated.

Leave the mixture in the Magimix bowl to cool. When cold add a few drops of vanilla essence and pour in the cream. Process until the mixture is smooth and creamy.

Pour the ice cream into a shallow container and freeze in the ice making compartment of a refrigerator or in a deep freeze until solid.

Banana cream

Serves 4

3 ripe bananas
100 g (4 oz) sugar

juice of 1 lemon
3 dl ($\frac{1}{2}$ pint) double cream

USE THE
METAL BLADE

Peel the bananas and process until smooth. Put puréed
bananas into a small saucepan with the sugar and lemon
juice and heat to boiling point, stirring to prevent
sticking. Leave to cool.

Whip the cream and fold it into the cold banana
mixture. Chill in a refrigerator before serving.

Pineapple cream

Serves 4

1 medium pineapple
100 g (4 oz) caster sugar

3 dl ($\frac{1}{2}$ pint) double cream

Peel and core the pineapple and roughly chop the flesh.

USE THE
METAL BLADE

Place the pineapple flesh in the Magimix bowl with the
bowl with the sugar and process until the pineapple is
reduced to a coarsely grained pulp. Remove the pulp.

USE THE
PLASTIC BLADE

Place the double cream in the Magimix bowl and process
until the cream begins to thicken. Add the pineapple and
continue to process for just long enough to mix the
ingredients.

Spoon into four goblets and chill for at least 1 hour
before serving.

Raspberry and yoghurt cream

Serves 4

450 g (1 lb) raspberries
6 dl (1 pint) yoghurt

1$\frac{1}{2}$ tablespoons demerara
sugar

USE THE
METAL BLADE

Reserve 12 raspberries and put the rest in the Magimix
bowl with the yoghurt and sugar. Process until the
mixture is smooth. Spoon into four glass goblets, top with
reserved raspberries and chill well before serving.

Note More sugar can be added if you find this a little
on the tart side – so much depends on the sweetness of the
raspberries.

215

Frozen raspberry whip

Serves 4

A quick, almost instant pudding to make when you are in a hurry.

*1 tablespoon gelatine
  powder
2 tablespoons lemon juice
75 ml (2½ fl. oz) boiling
  water*

*50 g (2 oz) sugar
2 egg whites
275 g (10 oz) frozen
  raspberries*

USE THE
METAL BLADE

Combine the gelatine powder, lemon juice, boiling water and sugar in the Magimix bowl and process for 40 seconds or until the gelatine has melted. Add the egg whites and continue to process for a further 10 seconds. With the machine switched on, add the raspberries, a few at a time, through the feed tube and process until the ingredients are well mixed. Turn into a wet mould and chill in a refrigerator for 2 hours until set firm.

Turn out and serve with double or whipped cream.

Iced liqueur mousse

Serves 6

*50 g (2 oz) shelled,
  blanched almonds
3 dl (½ pint) double cream
100 g (4 oz) icing sugar*

*4 tablespoons orange
  Curaçao, Grand Marnier
  or Drambuie
2 large egg whites*

USE THE
SLICING DISC

Slice the almonds with the slicing disc. Spread the almonds on a baking sheet and roast in a moderately hot oven (200°C, 400°F, Reg. 6) for about 3 minutes until golden brown.

USE THE
PLASTIC BLADE

Place the cream in the Magimix bowl with the sugar and liqueur and process until the cream has thickened (take care not to over-process).

Whip the egg whites until stiff. Add the egg whites to cream and switch the machine on and off to lightly incorporate the ingredients.

Divide the mixture between six glass goblets, sprinkle with the nuts and freeze in the ice-making compartment of a refrigerator or in a deep freeze for 3–4 hours. Transfer to the refrigerator for 30 minutes before serving.

216

Apple crisp

Serves 6

900 g (2 lb) cooking apples
3 tablespoons water
175 g (6 oz) granulated
  sugar
75 g (3 oz) bread with
  crusts removed

37 g (1½ oz) butter
2 tablespoons golden syrup
3 dl (½ pint) cream
50 g (2 oz) mixed peel

Peel, core and slice apples.

Combine apples, water and sugar in a heavy saucepan and cook over a medium heat until the apples are soft. Leave to cool.

Put the bread in the Magimix bowl and process into coarse breadcrumbs.

Melt the butter, add the breadcrumbs and fry over a medium heat until the breadcrumbs are crisp and golden brown. Add the syrup, mix well until the syrup melts and remove from the heat.

Put the apple mixture into the Magimix bowl, add the cream and process until the apple is smooth. Add mixed peel.

Place half the apple mixture in a glass serving dish, cover it with half the breadcrumb and syrup mixture and repeat the layers. Chill in a refrigerator for at least an hour before serving with cream.

Praline powder

150 g (5 oz) almonds
187 g (6½ oz) sugar

60 ml (2 fl. oz) water
pinch cream of tartar

Roast the almonds in a hot oven until golden brown.

Put the almonds into the Magimix bowl and process for a few seconds until roughly chopped.

Make a caramel sauce by combining the sugar, water and a pinch of cream of tartar in a small saucepan. Cook over a medium high heat stirring until the sugar has dissolved. Turn the heat up and boil hard until the mixture turns golden brown. Add the almonds to the caramel and mix. Pour the mixture onto buttered foil and leave to cool and set.

When the mixture is hard, break it into pieces and put in the Magimix bowl. Process until it is reduced to a rough powder. Store in an airtight jar and use as a topping for sweet soufflés, mousses and ice cream etc.

Magimix cheese cake

1 225 g (½ lb) packet
   digestive biscuits
100 g (4 oz) unsalted
   butter

225 g (8 oz) cream cheese
3 eggs
juice of 1 lemon
100 g (4 oz) caster sugar

USE THE
METAL BLADE

Break up the digestive biscuits and combine them with the butter, roughly chopped, in the Magimix bowl. Process until the butter and biscuits are well mixed. Scrape out the mixture and use it to line 20 cm (8 in.) flan case, pressing it evenly around the bottom and sides of the tin with the fingertips. Chill in a refrigerator while making the filling.

Combine the cheese, eggs, lemon juice and sugar in the Magimix bowl and process until the mixture is smooth and well mixed. Fill the flan case with the cheese mixture and bake in a moderate oven (180°C, 350°F, Reg. 4) for 30 minutes.

Serve cold.

Variations

Decorate the top of the cheesecake with halved strawberries.

Spread the bottom of the flan case with blackcurrant
or raspberry jam before adding the filling.

Index

TABLES OF WEIGHTS AND MEASURES

Below are tables of comparative weights and measurements to convert imperial recipe quantities into metric, and vice versa

Solid Measures

Exact conversions from imperial to metric do not usually give very convenient working quantities and so the larger metric measures here (as in the text) have been rounded off into units of 25 grammes.

Imperial	Recommended metric conversion
½ oz	12 grammes
¾	19
1	25
1½	37
2	50
3	75
4 (¼ lb)	100
6	175
8 (½ lb)	225
10	275
12 (¾ lb)	350
16 (1 lb)	450
1½ lbs	675
1¾ lbs	800
2 lbs	900

Liquid Measures

The millilitre is a very small unit of measurement and we felt that to use deci-litres (units of 1000 ml) would be better. This table gives some examples. *Note:* for quantities of 1¾ pints and over we have used litres and fractions of a litre.

Imperial	Recommended metric conversion
¼ pint	1.5 dl
⅓	2.1
½	3
¾	4.5
1	6
1¼	7
1½	9
1¾	10 (1 litre)
2	1.2 litres
2½	1.5 litres
3	1.8 litres

Oven Temperatures

Electricity		Gas	
Centigrade	Fahrenheit	Mark	Heat of Oven
130	250	1	Slow
150	300	2	Slow
170	325	3	Very moderate
180	350	4	Moderate
190	375	5	Moderately hot
200	400	6	Hot
220	425	7	Hot
230	450	8	Very hot
240	475	9	Very hot